for Todd,

Tino

Laura Roland Michundroy

A simple prayer,
a grateful wish,
that you enjoy
each special dish,
and feast upon
this glorious art,
with poetry
to warm your heart.

12/13/14

St. Martin

Designed and produced by Mary Wrigley and Richard James

Edited by Dr Susan Atchley and Alita Singh

Printed in the United States of America

ISBN: 978-0-692-32831-6

First Edition

Published By :

NORTH SOUTH NET, INC
CUSTOM CONTENT SOLUTIONS

6055 SW 85th Avenue
Miami, FL 33143
gduell@northsouthnet.com

Our heartfelt gratitude to:

Artemia Event Planners, Caribbean Liquors and Tobacco B.V., Island Real Estate Team, Lexwell Attorneys at Law, ORCO Bank, PDG,

PricewaterhouseCoopers, Prince Bernhard Cultural Foundation, Princess Juliana International Airport, Mrs. Kanta Ramchandani,

RBC Royal Bank N.V. St. Maarten, SZV Social and Health Insurances, The Daily Herald, UTS St. Maarten

awaken your senses

THE TEMPTATION RESTAURANT COOKBOOK

Chef Dino Jagtiani, Sir Roland Richardson, Laura Richardson

Photography Nataly Dannenberg

"A recipe has no soul, you as the cook must bring soul to the recipe" *Thomas Keller*

My greatest joy in the restaurant comes when I see a guest take that first bite of food, and then they look at their partner and give each other that "yes" nod as if to say in body language, "This food is delicious". Seeing that first reaction from people will never get old.

The rush I get comes from knowing I have contributed to someone's happiness, and is the reason I have chosen to write this book as I chose twelve wonderful years ago to open my restaurant: my passion for playing a role in the happiness of others.

Motivation for a chef blossoms in the opportunity to express him or herself freely via their culinary creations, or big mouth. Equally as thrilling for a chef is being in a position to influence the unity of mankind through the universal medium of food. Irrespective of politics, religion, gender or culture, the experiences that soulful meals provide create an undeniable connection across the globe. From the physical stimulation to the emotional awakening, no individual is naïve to the pleasures great food has to offer.

The task of facilitating this universal experience while exploring and honoring the varied canvases of cultures and palates presents an exciting challenge. Visual presentation, originality, and balance are all enhancing elements in a meal. However, flavor must rule above all else and ultimately ensures success with every cooking endeavour. The word "flavor" encompasses an infinite vocabulary of tastes, personified by the variety of terms used to characterize it: goût, sabor, maza, smak.

Our palates perceive not only sweet, salt, sour, bitter, spicy, but also textures such as the crunch of our Brulee'd Bananas in our "Banananana" dessert (page 103), the softness of avocado in my Sashimi Tuna (page 47), and temperature, such as the comforting warm slurp of Temptation's Onion Soup (page 37) or the refreshing cold of a Basil Lemon Drop cocktail (page 15) on a warm summer's day

... the experiences that soulful meals provide, create an undeniable connection across the globe

elements of taste, temperature and texture, all the while keeping in mind the varied gustatory preferences of individuals. Even the world's largest fast food restaurant chain appreciates the magic of such balance in their food menu options. Their signature hamburger carries taste (sweet onions, salty cheese, sour pickles, slightly bitter lettuce), texture (mild crunch of onions, crispy lettuce, soft bite of a baked bun) and temperature (warm charred meat, cool lettuce) all harmoniously present in each bite.

A playful yet elegant balance is what I strive to achieve in my cooking. Even delicate finishing touches such as a drizzle of olive oil, a sprinkling of herbs, a whimsical grating of cheese or a quick grind of peppercorns contribute toward creating the balance that will transform a chef's culinary work into a gastronomical masterpiece.

Those who know me, also know my affection for food. I remember as a child being pushed in the shopping trolley at "Food Center" admiring all the produce, eating raw peppers and smelling different herbs, while other children in the supermarket just cried and bugged their moms for candy. Fortunately I knew at a very young age that I was destined for a life in cooking. Even in pre-cable TV, and pre-Food Network days I remember being glued to the TV when Julia Child, Jacques Pepin, Martin Yan and singing Pasquale would strut their stuff on PBS. Would chefs really be rock stars today if it weren't for these pioneers?

St. Maarten, while not the foodie mecca that NYC is, definitely has its place in the "big leagues" of the culinary world. We are the gastronomic capital of the Caribbean, hands down! We are 37 square miles with over 300 restaurants, of which the top 10 could easily hold their own in any city on the planet.

Flamboyant Bouquet in Primary

Original Oil painted from life by Sir Roland Richardson

29.5 inches x 29 inches | December 2006 | Cupecoy, St. Maarten

We have incredible talent, diversity and, unique access to ingredients from all over the world. The same Prime cut steaks, freshly caught fish and boutique micro greens that find themselves on the menu in acclaimed big city eateries are dished up right here on our small island. Most of the time the chef, or host is also the owner of the restaurant. When was the last time you ate at a restaurant in a big city where the chef actually cooked for you? Or the owner of the restaurant actually waited on your table? Or served your bottle of wine? Or took your reservation on the phone? Or gave you a hug on your way in? Or, cracked a dirty joke with you? This is what defines island hospitality.

Where else in the world can you get Indian food cooked by a Haitian ...

St. Maarten's unique diverse melting pot community also contributes to our strong culinary reputation. Where else in the world can you eat Indian food, cooked by a Haitian, served by a Dominicana, listening to American rock 'n roll music, while a French baby sitter is looking after your half Chinese, half South African child at home?

Our variety of cuisines, from road-side grills affectionately called Lolo's, to Michelin star worthy high-end restaurants are all reflective of the passion and talent of this island's chefs, and foodies. While our unique style of hospitality, delicious culinary offerings, duty-free shopping and beautiful beaches, all contribute to making St. Maarten a sought-after vacation destination in the Caribbean, it is our colorful history that after all is why we are, who we are, today.

On November 11th, 1493, Christopher Columbus discovered this island, and named it St. Martin in homage to St. Martin of Tours. The island was rediscovered in the early 1600s and quickly was coveted by the French, Dutch, Spanish and English for its vast salt ponds, which the indigenous Indians had already named "Soualiga", Land of Salt.

Methodist Church, French Quarter
Hand-pulled etching by Sir Roland Richardson | Artist's proof | 12 inches x 9 inches | February 2001

in 1648, the French and Dutch governments settled the matter of ownership of the island with the signing of the Treaty of Concordia, and divided it in two parts, the French keeping the northern section, and the Dutch, the southern. The treaty recognized both the dual nationality and unity of the island, and stipulated that there would be no physical border between the two nations, and people, goods, and services would move freely. All provisions in the 1648 treaty are still enforced today. This spirit of amity set in the tone of this famous treaty is what led to St. Maarten being affectionately dubbed "The Friendly Island".

The 18th and 19th centuries were dominated by slavery and trade. Cattle, cotton, rum and salt were major economic drivers of our island, primarily managed by English settlers, and English became the dominant language. In the mid to late 1800s the abolishment of slavery resulted in a slumping economy. The island became a tax-free port due to its isolation and lack of resources. To this day, St. Maarten still enjoys the benefits of duty-free port status and, with over 100 nationalities represented here, English remains the native language.

During World War II, a small airstrip was built here by the US to protect the ships bringing oil from the refineries in South America, Aruba and Curaçao. When the war ended, the small landing field became St. Maarten's portal to the world and, Princess Juliana International Airport has since grown to become the most active airport in the region.

In the mid 1960s, the new tourism economy planted its first seeds here, the United States dollar gained great value, and St. Maarten, just hours from America, led visionaries like Dr Claude Wathey to develop a luxury tourist experience on "The Friendly Island". Which brings us to today, where luxury duty-free boutiques, culinary delights, pristine beaches and local charm, all contribute to welcoming over two million visitors, from all over the world, to our shores each year.

The fruit of St. Maarten's rich history and diversity is not only reflected in its cuisine. To celebrate this, I have collaborated with two other local artists, whose achievements and accolades speak for themselves – Sir Roland Richardson and his wife, Laura Richardson. The artwork on the cover was done expressly for this book. Sir Roland has achieved global acclaim and admiration from all realms of people for his work. His "Plein Air" paintings, all done from life, have been exhibited in over 100 one-man shows in galleries and museums, and now grace in this book for you to enjoy. Art students learn about him as the "Father of Caribbean Impressionism". You will enjoy admiring his paintings as they capture the essence of Caribbean life, and its exotic flora and fruits exemplified by Flamboyant trees in the iconic landscapes of this beautiful part of the world.

Complimenting and complementing his work is his wife's, Laura Richardson, who has a beautiful way with words that like a flower can bring a smile, or warm feeling to just about anyone. Her poetry is happy, breezy and eloquent just like the lady she is.

It is with great respect and admiration that the three of us decided to share proceeds from this book with two innovative and deserving foundations – *Be The Change* and *Art Saves Lives*. *Be The Change* was founded by Erika Cannegieter, who devoted her life to philanthropy. She challenged people who said they could not afford to give, by saying even if you give $1 you have made a difference. *Art Saves Lives* was founded by Nicole De Weever, to create opportunities for talented youngsters of our island to get exposure, training and guidance in the field of the performing arts. She herself rose to stardom, as a dancer, and made all of St. Maarten proud when she graced Broadway in a leading role in the musical *Fela!*. To call her a role model, inspiration and leader would simply be not be enough. We are delighted to share our passion and talent with you, and are honored that this book will find a place in our home and heart

The Calling of Color

"The world becomes visible only after light (which is invisible) transforms itself into color … first, as red, yellow and blue, then mixing together to become all the colors that enable us to see form, things.

The natural character of the three primary colors are clearly illustrated in this painting. The blue of the sky reflects space and depth, the yellow radiates, glows, and the red jumps forward.

Color is a dynamic force. The interaction, or the mixing of colors with each other allows us to see the form of things. In its dynamism, color also affects us by triggering thought and emotion. Our response to beauty is a response to color which comes out of light, which comes from the Divine." *Sir Roland Richardson*

Sapphire Flamboyant
Original "Plein Air" Oil painted on location from life
by Sir Roland Richardson
43 inches x 54 inches | July 2003 | Cupecoy, St. Maarten

Paul Peterson
Two time Gold Medal Winning Bartender | Taste of the Caribbean

Cocktails and Hors d'Oeuvres

Sint Martini

2oz | Vodka
1oz | Peach schnapps
1oz | Passion fruit juice
1oz | Cranberry juice

Combine all ingredients in a cocktail shaker with lots of ice, shake until frozen cold and strain into a chilled martini glass.

Basil Lemon Drop
aka Piña Verde

3oz | Lemon vodka
½oz | Fresh lemon juice
½oz | Basil syrup (*see recipe below)
2oz | Pineapple juice

Combine all ingredients in a cocktail shaker with lots of ice, shake until frozen cold and strain into a chilled martini glass.

* To make the basil syrup: Combine 1/2 cup sugar syrup and about 10 large fresh basil leaves in a small electric food chopper and purée until completely smooth. (Makes approximately 10 drinks)

Valentine's Day Champagne Cocktail

5oz	Chilled champagne
½ oz	Creme de cassis
½ oz	Creme de peach
1	Raspberry
1	Blueberry
1	Blackberry

This is our version of a Kir Royal and a Bellini mixed into one cocktail. Pour the champagne and the peach schnapps into a chilled champagne flute and carefully add the cassis so that it sinks to the bottom of the glass then add the berries.

Raspberry Rage

3oz	Raspberry vodka
½oz	Fresh lemon juice
½oz	Sugar syrup
1½oz	White cranberry juice
½ oz	Chambord

Combine all ingredients except Chambord in a cocktail shaker with lots of ice, shake until frozen cold and strain into a chilled martini glass. Next carefully add the Chambord so that it sinks to the bottom of the glass.

Cilantro Margarita

2 oz	Good quality Reposado tequila (we use Herradurra)
½ oz	Freshly squeezed lime juice
½ oz	Cointreau
½ oz	Agave syrup
1 tbs	Fresh cilantro leaves, or micro cilantro

In a cocktail shaker, combine all the ingredients and muddle the cilantro. Add ice and shake for 30 seconds. Pour this mixture into a glass and garnish with a wedge of lime.

The Perfect Martini

4 oz	Premium vodka or gin
½ oz or less	Dry vermouth
¼ oz	Olive brine (for a Dirty Martini)

Combine all ingredients in a full shaker of ice, shake vigorously for 15 seconds in order for ice shards to form. Serve in a chilled martini glass. Twist a strip of lemon peel and rub along the rim of the glass and add to martini or add three olives speared on a toothpick.

"What more proof need we of the bountifulness of God's promises than a mango tree in full fruit? Splendid, they dangle, as from the sky, on long orange yellow strings, swaying in constant movement to the rhythm of the Universe, bearing mangoes of many shapes and sizes and of endless, lovely colors.

Mangoes, Manna, Gifts from Heaven, reminiscent of Eden's Eternal Tree of Life."
Sir Roland Richardson

Grand Dangling Mangoes
Original "Plein Air" Oil
painted on location from life
by Sir Roland Richardson
78 inches x 120 inches
August 2008
Colombier, St. Martin

Tomato-Mozzarella-Balsamic Pipettes

Serves 4

as needed | Balsamic vinaigrette (see page 181)
4 | Cherry or grape tomatos
4 | Mini mozzarella balls
4 | Basil leaves

Fill each pipette with the balsamic dressing. Then skewer the tomato, mozzarella and basil.

Pipettes are easily available online.

I must give credit where credit is due. I enjoyed these delicious, and creative spin on tomato mozzeralla at a dear friend's wedding at the Ritz Carlton in South Beach. After eating the tomato and mozzeralla off the skewers, you squeeze the balsamic dressing into your mouth for a fun and appropriate pop of flavor.

Bruschettas
Serves 4

Crostinis

16 slices | Good quality bread such as baguette, pain de campagne or ciabatta

as needed | Extra virgin olive oil for coating the breads.

Generously brush the bread slices with olive oil and toast in the oven. Keep these crostinis until ready to use. They will hold for approx 1 hour.

Heirloom Tomato, Parmigiano and Micro Basil

¼ cup | An assortment of heirloom tomatoes sliced or quartered
(baby ones like cherry or grape)

2 tbs | Shaved Parmigiano Reggiano

8 sprigs | Micro basil

Top four crostinis with the above ingredients. Set aside until read to plate up and serve.

Brie–Apple–Caramelized Walnut

4 slices | Brie (same size as crostini)

¼ cup | Granny smith apple, brunoise cut

4 | Caramelized walnuts or pecans (see page 182)

Top each of four crostinis with a slice of brie, then top with the diced apple, and caramelized nuts. Set aside until ready to plate.

Bruschettas are fun and easy, don't limit yourself and restrict your own creativity. The key elements to a great bruschetta are great bread, good olive oil and well balanced flavors. These are some of my favorite combinations. But don't hold yourself back and try these alone, try beets, marscapone, flavored mayos, different cheeses and even fruits like figs and apricots. A drizzle of honey adds depth and punch.

Chickpea Masala, Sweet Potato and Pickled Ginger Chip

½ cup	Cooked chickpeas (or canned, properly drained and rinsed)
½ cup	Coconut curry sauce (see page 184)
½ cup	Sweet potato mash (see page 180)
4 slices	Pickled sushi ginger
as needed	Oil for frying
4 sprigs	Fresh cilantro

In a saucepan, over a medium heat, combine cooked chickpeas and curry sauce until heated through. Set aside. Deep fry the ginger slices in hot oil until crispy. Approximately 30 seconds. Drain on paper towel.

Top four crostinis with sweet potato mash, curried chickpeas and garnish with a ginger chip and a sprig of cilantro. Set aside until ready to plate.

Eggplant Hummus with Grilled Portabello

1	Eggplant	1 tbs	Fresh lemon juice	2 tbs	Balsamic vinaigrette (see page 181)
as needed	Olive oil	2 oz	Extra virgin olive oil		
as needed	Salt and pepper	1	Portabello mushroom		
1 clove	Garlic minced			4 sprigs	Arugula leaves

Pre-heat oven to 350°F. Cut eggplant in half, length wise. Brush with olive oil, and season with salt and pepper. Place in the oven, and roast until soft and slightly browned. Approximately 30 minutes. Immediately place in a container and cover to trap the steam. Let cool. Once cool, use a spoon to hollow out the pulp and combine with garlic, lemon juice, virgin olive oil, salt and pepper in a food processor. Set aside until ready to use. You will have extra to enjoy for another use.

Marinate the portabello with the balsamic vinaigrette, and place on the grill. Cook on both sides (approximately 10 minutes in total) until fully cooked, and soft. Slice portabello in thin even slices. Set aside until ready to use. Again you will have a little bit left over to enjoy for another use.

Spread some eggplant hummus on four crostinis, and layer the slices of grilled portabellos in a decorative way. Top with sprig of arugula leaf.

To plate: On a long rectangular plate, neatly arrange one of each of the brushettas in a row

Shrimp Fried Rice
Makes 8

8	Shrimps (16-20 size)
as needed	Salt and pepper
as needed	Olive oil
as needed	Asian grilling glaze (see page 179)

Pre-heat your grill. Peel, and devein the shrimp. Season with olive oil, salt and pepper. Grill for approximately one minute per side, brushing the glaze on both sides. Set aside, and keep warm until ready to use.

Fried Rice
Makes 1½ cups

as needed	Olive oil
1 tsp	GGS (ginger, garlic, scallion)
½ cup	Mixed Asian veggies, like bok choy, carrots, shiitake mushrooms, celery, bean sprouts, snow peas (all finely julienned)
1 oz	Ketchap Manis (Indonesian soy sauce)
2 oz	Chicken broth
1 cup	Pre-cooked rice (basmati works well)

In a sauté pan or wok, over high heat add oil, GGS and mixed vegetables. Stir fry for two minutes, then add Ketchap Manis and chicken broth. Let the vegetables simmer until cooked, and liquid is almost disolved. Add the rice and stir fry until combined.

To plate: On a small Chinese soup spoon, place some stir fried rice on the bottom and top with a grilled shrimp. Sprinkle with black and white sesame seeds. Garnish with a sprig of cilantro.

The perfect combo of sweet, sour, salty, bitter, umami, soft, crispy, hot and cold - all in one bite. The Chinese spoon has changed the landscape of cocktail parties everywhere - and with that, always making this a hit.

Middle Eastern Spiced Lamb Sliders
on Mini Brioche with Caramelized Shallot Aioli

Serves 4

1 lbs	Ground lamb
½	Onion (grated)
1 tsp	Ground cumin
2 tsp	Ground coriander
½ tsp	Cinnamon and allspice
Pinch	Cayenne pepper (optional)
4 tbs	Fresh mint, parsley and cilantro (finely chopped)
as needed	Salt and pepper

In a mixing bowl, combine all the ingredients. Shape into golf ball size meat balls, and press down to mini burger patties. You can sauté or grill these patties to your desired doneness. They will cook rather quickly, 2-3 minutes in total.

Caramelized Shallot Aioli (Burger Sauce)

1 cup	Dijon mustard
1 cup	Mayonnaise
½ cup	Shallot marmalade (see page 182)

Mix all ingredients, and set aside until ready to use. This can be stored in a squeeze bottle in the fridge for up to two weeks. This sauce is also great on steaks, lamb chops and pork chops.

Gourmet burgers are becoming all the rage these days. From Kobe beef, to all natural, to custom ground beef or even going away from beef as we do here with lamb. My tip for a super burger is always grind, season and shape the burger patties yourself. Then remember all the elements of taste - sweet, sour, salty, bitter, hot, cold, crispy, soft - and try to get that all happening in one bite.

Crispy Fried Shallots

    2 | Shallots (thinly sliced)
as needed | Rice flour, salt and pepper
as needed | Oil for deep frying set at 350°F

Dredge the shallots rings in the seasoned rice flour. Deep fry them for 30-40 seconds. Drain on paper towels.

To assemble the lamb sliders you will need:

    8 | Mini brioche buns (halved and warmed) (ask your favorite bakery)
1 cup | Baby arugula
8 slices | Heirloom tomato

Place a small dollop of burger sauce (caramelized shallot aioli) on each half of the bun. On the top half, place a few leaves of arugula and a slice of tomato. On the bottom half of the bun, place the cooked lamb patty. Arrange them nicely on a serving platter, and get ready to be the hit of any party.

Fish Cleaning at the Market
Hand-pulled etching by Sir Roland Richardson | Artist's proof | 5 inches x 8 inches | 2009

Salt Fish 'n Johnny Cakes

Serves 4

Johnny Cakes

2 cups	Flour		¼ cup	Vegetable oil
2 tsp	Baking powder		as needed	Warm water
2 tsp	Salt		as needed	Oil for frying
2 tsp	Sugar			

> "Who is a real St. Martiner" is a popular local debate, with many opinions about who is considered to be "from hyah!" From being born here, to having ancestral roots, to having been legally or illegally naturalized here, to just having a sweet spot in your heart for St. Maarten. I say lets settle this once and for all and establish a gauge, "anyone, who has never eaten Salt Fish 'n Johnny Cakes" cannot call themselves a St. Martiner.

Combine flour, baking powder, salt, sugar and vegetable oil in a bowl. Mix with a fork until the mixture resembles a coarse meal. Add enough warm water to form a smooth dough. Knead the dough for five minutes, and let the dough rest for one hour. Roll the dough into golf ball sized balls, and then flatten them into little disks. Deep fry 2-3 minutes until the dough is fully cooked through. Keep warm until ready to use.

Salt Fish

2 fillets	Salted cod		1 cup	Tomatoes (diced)
as needed	Olive oil		½ cup	Water
½ cup	Onion (diced)		½ cup	Garlic butter (cold, cut in cubes)
½ cup	Red bell pepper (diced)		½ cup	Parsley (chopped)
½ cup	Green bell pepper (diced)		as needed	Salt and pepper
½ cup	Scallions thinly (sliced)			

Rinse the salt off the cod and boil for two hours, replacing the water two times. Taste the fish to make sure most of the saltiness has been eliminated. Flake the fish, and set aside until ready to use.

In a sauté pan, on high heat, add the olive oil, onions, peppers, scallions and tomatoes. Cook the mixture until the flavors are released. Add the water, and simmer until the vegetables are cooked. Add the garlic butter and parsley, and adjust seasoning with salt and pepper. Finally add the salt fish, and mix until all is combined.

There is no right way to eat this, but I like to make mini sandwiches with the Johnny Cakes

Spicy Tuna on Arroz Pegao (Crispy Rice)

with Garlic Sprouts, and Avocado

Serves 4

4 cups	Prepared sushi rice (see page 38)
as needed	Canola oil for frying
1 lbs	Sashimi grade tuna small diced
½ cup	Mayonnaise
as needed	Siracha hot sauce (as desired to your "spicy" taste)
2 tbs	Prepared soy-ginger sauce (page 187)
½ cup	Scallions (finely chopped)
1 tbs	Truffle oil
1 tsp	Prepared wasabi
16 slices	Pickled ginger
as needed	Freshly ground black pepper

Using your favorite mold – round, square, oblong etc – mold rice into the shape of mold so it looks like a rice cake, approximately ¾ inch in height. While handling sushi rice it is necessary to wet your finger tips to prevent the rice from sticking.

In a large sauté pan, over medium to high heat, panfry rice cake on both sides until golden brown and crispy. Drain on paper towels and keep warm.

Meanwhile, in a medium mixing bowl, combine tuna, mayo, siracha, soy ginger sauce, scallions, truffle oil and mix well to combine. It is important to keep the mixture super cold. So refrigerate if you are making this ahead.

Top rice cakes with spicy tuna mixture using same mold so that the tuna and rice cake are the same size.

Top with diced avocado and garlic sprouts. Serve with traditional sushi condiments

Sushi Rice

Yields 4 cups cooked

2 cups	Sushi or short grain rice
2 cups	Water, plus extra for rinsing
4 tbs	Rice vinegar
2 tbs	Sugar
1 tbs	Kosher salt

Using a mixing bowl and strainer, rinse and drain the sushi rice 3 times or until the water runs clear. Combine the 2 cups of rinsed rice with the 2 cups of water in a rice cooker, and cook according to the settings on the machine.

Combine the rice vinegar, sugar and salt, and mix until completely dissolved. Essentially you are seasoning the vinegar.

Using a special wooden Hangiri (Japanese wooden bowl) immediately cool the rice by fanning it down while mixing in the rice vinegar mixture. This is the most crucial step in sushi rice making. The rice should be cooled to just a slightly warm temperature. Part of the sushi eating experience is to have slightly warm rice with ice cold fish.

Once cooled, the rice is ready to use. It should be used up within 24 hours.

In Latin cooking, "Arroz Pegao" refers to rice that gets stuck at the bottom of the pan. This crispy, toasty, golden brown rice is usually enjoyed by the lucky people who end up having to wash the pot. Here, we intentionally re-create that crispy goodness by pan frying the rice cake and topping it with a spicy tuna mixture.

I've given a recipe for sushi rice and encourage you to try making it at home, but keep in mind that making sushi rice is an art that is mastered over years in Japan. If you're successful, you'll have serious culinary bragging rights. Alternatively go to your favorite sushi restaurant, and ask them for 2 cups of prepared rice so that you can have a mini sushi party at home. It helps if you bring your own container.

"An image speaks volumes. Fish was our daily form of food growing up in Grand Case in the 1950s. Money was rare, sometimes services and help was paid for with a strap of fish.

The composition of the strap was by no means accidental but deliberate. As different people like different fish, the strap assured that you got what you liked but mixed with others so that everyone was sure to get something they preferred.

Here we have different fish, each a different color, each a different flavor and in the absence of a scale to weigh the fish, the proportions were always generous."
Sir Roland Richardson

A Strap of Fish
Original Oil painted from life
by Sir Roland Richardson
33inches x 21inches | 2009

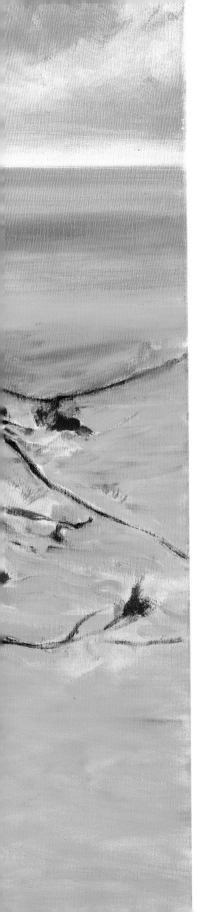

Without Complaint

The clouds pass by
without complaint,
the sun does rise
without constraint.
The sea resigns,
then flows back in,
the flora bloom
as days begin.
We earn from these
eternal things,
a simple peace
that nature brings,
beyond all thought
and strategy
a quiet, endless,
mystery.

Poem by Laura Richardson

Baie Longe Colors III
Fine art limited edition
from an Original "Plein Air" Oil
painted on location from life
by Sir Roland Richardson

"Real men wear aprons"

Appetizers

44 | **Seafood Martini**
Tuna, Crab and Salmon tossed in our Ceviche Marinade, and topped
with Grilled Shrimp, Fried Plantain Chips and Avocado

46 | **Seared Foie Gras with Balsamic Jelly**
Poached Pears, Cranberry Chutney and Puff Pastry

51 | **Temptation's Onion Soup**
spiked with Beer and Brandy

52 | **Lobster Salad**
with Lemon Mayo, Celery, Apples, Dill and Tarragon

54 | **Spinach-Ricotta Ravioli**
with Fricassee of Chanterelle, Porcini and Button Mushrooms

56 | **Grilled Peach Salad**
with Crumbled Roquefort Cheese, Caramelized Pecans and Balsamic Vinaigrette

59 | **Hot 'n' Cold Soup**
Cuban Style Black Bean Soup and Chilled Gazpacho coupled together
with a Goat Cheese Empanada

62 | **Sashimi Tuna**
with Soy-Ginger, Truffle Oil, Lemon-Lime, Avocado, Cucumbers and Plantain

67 | **Goat Cheese Bon Bons**
with Grapefruit, Sunflower Seeds, Candied Ginger and Rosemary Honey

68 | **Crab Beignets**
with Chipotle Mayo and Tomato-Red Onion Salsa

71 | **Caesar Salad**
in an Edible Parmesan Bowl with Toasted Pine Nuts

Seafood Martini

Tuna, Crab and Salmon tossed in our Ceviche Marinade, and topped with Grilled Shrimp, Fried Plantain Chips and Avocado

Serves 4

½ cup	Sashimi quality tuna (diced small)
½ cup	Crab
½ cup	Fresh salmon (diced small)
½ cup	Fresh red snapper (diced small)
½ cup	Freshly squeezed lemon juice
½ cup	Freshly squeezed lime juice
1 cup	Freshly squeezed orange juice
1tbs	Fresh ginger minced
1 tbs	Honey
¼ cup	Coconut milk
¼ cup	Fresh cilantro leaves picked
½ cup	Red onion (very thinly sliced)
4	Jumbo shrimp
as needed	Olive oil
as needed	Salt and pepper
8 pieces	Plantain chips
¼ cup	Freshly diced avocado

In a mixing bowl, set over ice, combine tuna, crab, salmon and snapper. Keep over ice bath in the refrigerator until ready to use. Make the ceviche dressing by combining the lemon, lime and orange juices, ginger, honey, coconut milk and cilantro. Keep the dressing very cold.

Approximately 20-30 minutes before you wish to serve the ceviche, mix the dressing with the diced seafood, and the red onions. Serve in a martini glass, and garnish with the plantain chips, and diced avocado.

Ceviche is a great "hot weather", refreshing, trendy, appetizer originally from Peru. There are endless options with ceviche for a cook to express his or her own creativity. Some great ideas to add into this mixture would be grapefruit, watermelon, pumpkin seeds, tomatoes, sweet potato, chipotle, corn and dill. The key to a great ceviche is, in my opinion, to serve it ice cold.

Seared Foie Gras with Balsamic Jelly
Poached Pears, Cranberry Chutney, and Puff Pastry

Serves 4

Balsamic Jelly

2 cups	Balsamic vinegar
2 grams	Gelatin Sheets
as needed	Ice water

Place the balsamic vinegar into a small saucepan and reduce by half over medium-low heat, approximately 30 minutes. Let cool until slightly warm. Bloom the gelatin sheets by soaking them in ice water and then remove from ice water and squeeze excess moisture. Add to warm balsamic reduction and mix thoroughly until all of the gelatin sheets have melted throughout. Pour into a plastic lined shallow container (or silicone mold) and let set up in a refrigerator until firm, approximately 40 minutes. Once set, cut into cubes and hold until needed.

Poached Pears

2	Pears
as needed	Port wine (enough to cover the pears in the pot)
1tbs	Orange zest
1	Star anise, and cinnamon stick
½ cup	Red wine vinegar

Peel, core, and cut the pears into six wedges. Place in a saucepan, and add rest of the ingredients. Bring to a simmer, and continue to poach the pears until they are fork tender. Remove the pears, and reduce the poaching liquid until it is the consistency of maple syrup. Place the pears back inside the reduced poaching liquid, and hold warm until ready to use.

We have done several versions of foie gras over the last ten years, from figs, pears, apples, apricots and cranberries to brioche and puff pastry etc... however, everytime I take this off the menu, people simply request it "the old way"!!!

The bright and tart acidity of the balsamic jelly and cranberry chutney give a much needed contrast to the richness of the foie and the sweetness of the poached pears and the crisp and buttery puff pastry lend a contrasting crunch!

Cranberry Chutney

1 bag	Frozen cranberries (12 oz)	1 cup	Honey
2 cups	Orange juice	2 springs	Fresh rosemary, finely chopped
1/2 cup	Balsamic vinegar		

Combine all ingredients in a sauce pan and bring to a simmer over medium heat. Let simmer until cranberries burst and liquid is reduced and the sauce is thickened. Let chutney cool and store until ready to use.

Puff Pastry Bouche

1 sheet	Puff pastry (store bought, partially thawed)
1	Egg (beaten)
3 tbs	Water
1 tbs	Sea salt

Pre-heat oven to 375°F. Lay the puff pastry on a clean sheet pan or work surface. Prepare eggwash by whisking the egg and the water together. Using a cookie cutter to cut 3 inch round circles of puff pastry, and place them on a baking sheet. Brush with eggwash, and sprinkle with sea salt. Bake in the oven approximately 12 minutes until the dough puffs up and has nice golden brown color.

Seared Foie Gras

| 4 slices | Foie gras (best quality "extra") (approximately 2 oz each) |
| as needed | Salt and pepper |

Season the foie gras slices with salt and pepper. Place in a hot pan and sear on one side for approximately 30 seconds. Lower the temperature to medium low and flip. Gently cook until the foie gras is warmed through. While it cooks, baste the foie with its rendered fat. Let it sit for at least two minutes in the pan, off the heat, before plating.

To plate: Spoon a small dollop of the cranberry chutney onto the center of the plate. Gently place the puff pastry bouche on top of the chutney and top with three slices of the poached pears, then the foie gras, and garnish with the balsamic gelee. Drizzle some of the reduced "gastrique" (the reduced poaching liquid) on the plate in a decorative pattern.

**Still Life with
Flamboyant and
Bougainvillea
on Artist's
Worktable**
Original Oil
painted from life
by Sir Roland Richardson
60 inches x 41 inches
September 2009

Temptation's Onion Soup
spiked with Beer and Brandy

Serves 4

as needed	Butter and olive oil
1	Vidalia onion (thinly sliced)
1	Spanish onion (thinly sliced)
½ cup	Beer (amber or dark if available)
½ cup	Cognac
2 oz	Honey
1 tsp	Dried thyme
1	Bay leaf
6 cups	Chicken stock or low sodium chicken broth
1 cup	50% reduced veal stock
as needed	Salt and pepper
4 slices	Left over, or toasted French or Italian bread
1 cup	Gouda cheese (grated)
1 cup	Gruyere cheese (grated)

I don't believe in having signature dishes, I believe all my menu items are like my children, and therefore it's not morally correct to choose a favorite dish. But, if we ever did have one, this would be it. This is by far the most requested recipe we get from patrons. Working on an island with so many talented French chefs, and with the knowledge that French onion soup is one of those dishes iconic to French cuisine, it took me a lot of courage to put this on the menu, as I knew it would be constantly compared to every other French onion soup. Take the time to caramelize the onions properly, and make sure you have a rich flavorful broth. This is so hearty it can be a meal in itself.

In a large rondeau or saucepan, over a high heat, add the butter, olive oil and onions. Caramelize the onions, while stirring constantly. (This is the secret to the soup). The onions should develop a really good brown color. This process, if done correctly will take at least 45 minutes. Deglaze with the cognac and beer, making sure to scrape off all the bits on the bottom of the pan. (This is called "le fond", and it is loaded with flavor!) Add the honey, thyme, bay leaf and both stocks. Simmer until the soup is reduced by 30%. Adjust seasoning if you have to with salt and pepper.

51

Pour soup in bowls, top with bread and cheese, and bake in a 450°F oven for approximately 10 minutes until the cheese is nicely gratineed. Let rest for a couple of minutes as soup will

Lobster Salad

with Lemon Mayo, Celery, Apples, Dill and Tarragon

Serves 4

2 | Lobster tails (meat removed, and diced into bite size pieces. Reserve the shells for presentation.)

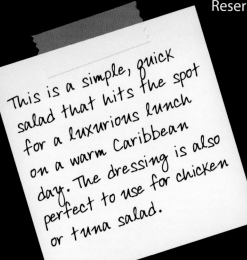

This is a simple, quick salad that hits the spot for a luxurious lunch on a warm Caribbean day. The dressing is also perfect to use for chicken or tuna salad.

Court Bouillon

1 qt | Court Bouillon
(flavorful cooking liquid for poaching seafood)

1 qt | Water

1 cup | White wine

¼ | Rib of celery and onion

1 sprig | Thyme

1 | Bay leaf

½ | Lemon

Bring ingredients to a boil and strain. This is now ready for poaching fish and shellfish.

First blanch the lobster shells in the Court Bouillon until bright red. Remove and store in the fridge to cool. Next poach the lobster meat for 6-8 minutes until just barely cooked. Do not overcook. Let cool in the refrigerator for 2 to 3 hours, or until completely cooled down.

Dressing

1 cup | Mayonnaise

2 | Lemons (juiced and zested)

¼ cup | Celery, apple and red onion (brunoised or small diced)

¼ cup | Equal amounts of fresh tarragon, fresh dill and fresh parsley (roughly chopped)

In a mixing bowl combine all ingredients.

To plate: Combine the lobster and the dressing, and stuff back into the shells. Serve on a bed of lightly dressed mixed greens.

the spinach, ricotta, Parmigiano cheese, egg and freshly grated nutmeg. Adjust seasoning with salt and pepper.

Lay the wonton skins on a clean work surface. Place 2 tsp of filling in the center of each wonton. Brush two edges with egg wash and fold over to form a triangle. If using circle shaped wonton skins, fold over to create a half moon or cresent shape. Place the ravioli on a sheet tray dusted with corn meal until ready to use. These can be prepared 1 to 3 days ahead.

Place the ravioli in boiling salted water. They will cook in less then two minutes. When they float to the surface they are done. Remove from the boiling water using a slotted spoon and then place in the sauté pan with the mushroom sauce. Gently toss the ravioli and sauce together, until heated through.

To plate: In a beautiful pasta bowl, place the ravioli in the center of the plate. Place some of the mushrooms from the sauce neatly around and on top of the ravioli. Spoon some of the sauce over the plate. Garnish with fresh tarragon, fresh basil, basil oil, and shaved Parmigano Reggiano.

We use wonton skins here for two reasons. Firstly they are time saving, and secondly they really give this dish a delicate, light almost airy mouth feel that is simply unattainable with traditional methods. For this reason, I enjoy pairing this with a heavy sauce of porcinis, cream, truffle oil and Parmigiano cheese.

Grilled Peach Salad
with Crumbled Roquefort Cheese, Caramelized Pecans and Balsamic Vinaigrette

Serves 4

2	Peaches
as needed	Sugar (to dredge the peaches)
6 cups	Mixed field greens
½ cup	Crumbled Roquefort cheese
½ cup	Caramelized pecans (see page 182)
¼ cup	Balsamic vinaigrette (see page 181)

Cut peaches in half and remove the pit. Cut each half into four wedges, so each peach will yield 8 wedges. Dredge the peaches in sugar, and place on the grill for one minute on each side, just to get them a little caramelized

In a mixing bowl, add the field greens, cheese, pecans and vinaigrette. Gently toss all ingredients.

To plate: Place a neat mound of salad on the center of plate and arrange the slices of peaches randomly and abstractly on top of the salad.

Tossing the peaches in sugar, and then grilling them gives a nice caramelization which really balances the acidity of the vinaigrette, as well as giving a slight warmth to the chilled greens. This salad is delicious, easy and guaranteed to impress. Some salad tips: Use the best mixture of greens you can find, and don't over do it with the dressing. If you are not a peach or bleu cheese lover, use any cheese, fruit or nut combo.

Hot 'n' Cold Soup

Cuban Style Black Bean Soup and Chilled Gazpacho coupled together
with a Goat Cheese Empanada

Serves 4

Goat Cheese Empanadas | Pate Brisee (Pie Dough)

1 1/3 cup	Flour
1 stick (4oz)	Butter
pinch	Salt and sugar
2 oz	Ice cold water
8 tsp	Goat cheese
as needed	Egg wash (1egg with 1tbs water beaten)
as needed	Oil for deep frying

Place flour, butter, salt and sugar in food processor. Pulse until you have a course crumbly mixture. Add water and pulse just until dough forms a ball. Let the dough rest for 20 minutes. Then roll out into a 9 inch circle. Using a cookie cutter, make 2 or 3 inch mini circles. You will have extra dough to use for another use. Fill each circle with 2 tsp of goat cheese and brush one half of the outer edge of the circle with egg wash. Fold together to form a half-moon shaped empanada. You can crimp the edges with a fork for decoration, and to seal properly. Deep fry the empanadas in pre-heated 350°F oil for approximately one minute, until golden brown.

The idea of doing two soups in the same bowl came when I was on externship and saw New England and Manhattan Clam Chowders served side by side in the same bowl. This version makes more sense because the two soups actually complement each other, both having Latin influences. The hot and cold contrast takes this to another level. I truly believe this is one of my most creative dishes ever.

Gazpacho

3 cups	Vine ripened tomatoes roughly chopped
1 cup	Red bell pepper roughly chopped
1 cup	Onion roughly chopped
1 cup	Cucumber roughly chopped
1 clove	Garlic
3 tbs	Red wine vinegar
3 tbs	Extra virgin olive oil
½ bunch	Fresh cilantro
as needed	Chilled ice water, and chilled tomato juice
as needed	Salt and pepper
½	Fresh lime

In a blender purée the tomatos, peppers, onion, cucumbers, garlic, vinegar, olive oil and cilantro into a paste. When ready to serve, thin down with ice water and chilled tomato juice. Adjust seasoning with salt and pepper, and a squeeze of lime.

Black Bean Soup

1 cup	Chopped bacon
as needed	Olive oil
1 cup	Onions roughly chopped
2 cloves	Garlic roughly chopped
½ bunch	Cilantro
3 cups	Black beans
6 cups	Water
1 cup	Coconut milk
as needed	Salt and pepper

Sauté the bacon in olive oil until some of the fat renders. Add the onions, garlic, cilantro and cook for 2-3 minutes until the flavors have been released. Add the black beans and water, and cook until the beans are soft. (Approximately two hours). Keep adding more water if too much has evaporated. Once the beans are cooked, add the coconut milk. Blend the mixture and season with salt and pepper.

Note: It is OK to use canned beans for this, although it is not ideal. If using canned beans, make sure they are well rinsed, and do not use any of the liquid from the can. This will cut the cooking time down to 15-20 minutes.

Using two ladels or two teapots a lip for pouring.

Sashimi Tuna
with Soy-Ginger, Truffle Oil, Lemon-Lime, Avocado, Cucumbers and Plantain

Serves 4

1 lbs	Sashimi grade tuna (best quality is imperative here)
½ cup	Truffle oil (either store bought, or make your own with truffle peelings and olive oil
¼ cup	Freshly squeezed lime and lemon juices
¼ cup	Soy ginger sauce (see page 187)
1	Avocado (sliced)
1 cup	Cucumber (julienned or sliced on mandolin)
12	Plantain chips (either store bought or home made)

With your sharpest knife, cut the tuna into a neat square block. Reserve the trim for another use, like tuna salad or spicy tuna (see page 37). Cut thin slices of tuna and lay them neatly on a chilled plate.

If you have squeeze bottles, then fill three of them up separately with the soy-ginger sauce, the lemon-lime juice and truffle oil. Neatly arrange the cucumber and avocado on top of the tuna, and lightly drizzle with the three sauces. Garnish with plantain chips.

On a trip to NYC, I had the opportunity to spend a couple of days in the kitchens of Sushi Samba. I am so embarrassed how easy this is, and that I didn't create something like this on my own. I love this appetizer so much, that it becomes my dinner of choice more than a couple of times per week. I cannot stress how important it is to source the highest quality tuna available, as you will be eating this raw. Make sure it is of sashimi quality, with at least a #1 grading.

Crab Beignets
with Chipotle Mayo and Tomato-Red Onion Salsa

Serves 6

Crab Beignets

1 lbs	Lump crab
½ cup	Apple (small diced)
½ cup	Red onion (small diced)
½ cup	Celery (small diced)
½ cup	Fresh parsley (finely chopped)
½ cup	Mayonnaise
½ cup	Bread crumbs
as needed	Salt and pepper
as needed	Flour, eggs and panko (for breading)
as needed	Oil for frying pre-heated to 350°F

In a mixing bowl, combine crab, apples, red onions, celery, parsley and mayonnaise. Essentially you are making a crab salad. Then add enough bread crumbs so that the mixture binds together.

Shape the crab mixture into 2 inch balls. Let the balls cool so that they firm up nicely. This will make them easier to handle during breading. Bread the crab beignets using standard breading procedures (flour, eggs, breadcrumbs). When ready to serve, deep fry the crab beignets until golden brown. Drain on paper towel.

To plate: Using a squeeze bottle, make a zig zag pattern of the chipotle mayo. Then place three crab beignets neatly in a row. Top with the salsa, and garnish with a cilantro sprig.

Crab is such a versatile canvas for so many options, you can go Asian, Latin, Mediterranean, Indian, etc ... here we make a chipotle sauce and hit it with a tart tomato-red onion salsa. By all means don't limit yourself with this recipe. Feel free to add your own signature on this.

Aioli

2 tbs	Puréed Chipotle in adobo
1 cup	Mayonnaise
2 tbs	Lime juice
2 tbs	Honey
¼ cup	Fresh cilantro

Combine ingredients into a blender and purée until smooth with a sauce-like consistency. Chill and reserve.

Salsa

1 cup	Tomato (small diced)
½ cup	Red onion (small diced)
½ cup	Cucumber (small diced)
½ cup	Fresh cilantro chopped
¼ cup	Freshly squeezed lime juice
as needed	Salt and pepper

Combine ingredients in a bowl, mix well, chill and reserve.

Goat Cheese Bon Bons
with Grapefruit, Sunflower Seeds, Candied Ginger and Rosemary Honey

8 oz	Goat cheese (well chilled)		3 sprigs	Fresh rosemary leaves (picked)
as needed	All purpose flour		½ cup	Honey
as needed	Eggs (beaten)		1	Grapefruit (segments removed)
as needed	Panko bread crumbs		¼ cup	Sunflower seeds or pumpkin seeds
as needed	Oil for frying (350°F)		2 pieces	Candied or crystallized ginger
½ cup	Orange juice			finely chopped

Place flour, eggs and panko in three separate bowls. Wet your hands with some water and make 1 inch balls of the goat cheese using the same technique as for making meat balls. Bread the goat cheese balls according to standard breading procedures (flour, egg, breadcrumbs).

Deep fry the breaded goat cheese for 1 minute until golden brown.

Combine the orange juice, rosemary and honey in a blender.

To plate: Place three balls of warm goat cheese in the center of a shallow plate. Place two grapefruit segments on either side and then drizzle with the rosemary honey. Sprinkle some pumpkin seeds, and candied ginger.

This appetizer could also be a dessert or cheese course. Use any combo of berries, fruit and/or nuts. Poached pears or figs will also work wonderfully with these light airy, soft fried goat cheese balls.

67

Curried Beef Tacos

with Coconut Rice, Avocado-Black Bean Salsa

Serves 4

as needed	Olive oil
1 cup	Onion (small diced)
½ cup	Red bell pepper
1 tsp	Minced garlic and ginger
½ cup	Tomato concasse (diced tomatoes, skin and seeds removed)
1 tsp	Tomato paste
1 tsp	Chipotle (minced with adobo sauce)
1 lbs	Beef for stewing (very small diced) (we use tenderloin tips or trimmings)
1 cup	Curry sauce (page 184)
1	"Indian bouquet garni" (see below)
½ cup	Coconut milk
as needed	Fresh cilantro, salt, and pepper

Heat olive oil in a large sauté pan, add onions, bell peppers, ginger, garlic, tomato, tomato paste, chipotle and beef. Sauté until aromas are released. Add curry sauce, and adjust the heat to low. Continue to simmer until beef is tender (approximately 45 minutes to an hour). In a separate pot, over medium heat, infuse coconut milk with the bouquet garni flavors. Add flavored coconut milk to curried beef. Adjust seasoning with salt and pepper, and sprinkle fresh cilantro on top.

Taco Shells

8	Wonton wrappers
as needed	Oil for deep frying

Using a taco shell mold or tongs, fry wonton skins into mini taco shells. Place on paper towels to drain. Keep warm.

Avocado-Black Bean Salsa

1	Avocado (small diced)
1/2 cup	Cooked black beans
1/2 cup	Red onion, red pepper, tomato (small diced)
½	Lime (juiced)
2 tbs	Fresh cilantro (rough chopped)
as needed	Salt and pepper

Combine all ingredients into a bowl. Keep in the refrigerator.

Coconut Rice

1 cup	Pre-cooked basmati rice
2 tbs	Minced scallions
¼ cup	Coconut milk
½ tsp	Sugar
as needed	Salt, pepper and sesame seeds

In a sauce pan over medium heat, combine rice with scallions, coconut milk, salt, pepper, sugar, and sesame seed. Stir over medium heat or until rice is warmed.

To plate: Make 2 little mounds of rice on plate. Fill each taco shell with beef mixture and lean it against the rice. Top with avocado-black bean salsa.

Indian Bouquet Garni

1	Cheese cloth cut into 4 inch square
1	Cinnamon stick
3	Cardamom pods
6	Black peppercorns
1 inch	Piece of ginger

Place all ingredients in the center of cheese cloth and tie up by bring all four corners together. Use this to flavor sauces, stews or braised dishes.

This is my contribution to "Gourmet Street Food". Although, I hate using the word fusion to describe a cuisine, this Indian-Latin blend of flavors actually makes sense. Both cuisines feature many of the same ingredients such as onions, garlic, tomatoes, rice, coconut, cilantro, limes, cumin, cinnamon, chilies, beans etc. This "Taco" is a real crowd pleaser and draws many repeat customers. Feel free to use lamb, chicken, pork or goat instead of beef.

Caesar Salad
in an edible Parmesan Bowl with Toasted Pine Nuts
Serves 4

Parmesan Bowls

3 cups | Grated parmesan cheese

In a hot non-stick pan, over high heat, sprinkle the cheese evenly all over the pan. Turn the fire to low, and let the cheese toast, or almost burn. Check to see when the bottom side is done. Then, working quickly, remove the cheese and turn onto an upside down bowl and let the cheese cool. After a few minutes, as it cools, it becomes hard. Carefully remove the parmesan bowl and you are now ready to fill it with your Caesar salad.

Salad

1 head | Romaine lettuce, finely chopped
½ cup | Caesar dressing (see page 185)
¼ cup | Toasted pine nuts
½ cup | Shaved Parmigiano Reggiano

In a bowl combine all the ingredients, and gently toss. Place the leaves neatly inside the bowl. Garnish with freshly ground black pepper, or add grilled chicken, shrimp or your favorite Caesar add on.

I haven't figured out why Caesars have such a broad appeal all over the world. Who would think that romaine lettuce, anchovies, raw eggs, lemon and parmigiano cheese would have such a cult following. Even in Temptation with so many creative options, the Caesar "from next door" continues to be the most popular appetizer we offer. Proves we are all creatures of habit.

"This is the last remaining intact sugar plantation-era estate on St. Martin. Situated at the center of the island, in the valley at the foot of Pic Paradis, our highest hills, next to the village of Colombier. It has been in the care of my family since the 1700s when it was known as Golden Grove Plantation. Today we call it Colombier, and sometimes "the Country." Still a farm, this lovely property allows a window to the natural beauty and graciousness of our homeland. As if imagined, it is a living tableau constantly changing, yet eternal; a romantic oleander-lined driveway, through a lush, luminous pasture, past a coconut grove to a secret place with immense ancient trees and a view of the hills rolling down to the Caribbean Sea. There are seasons when it can only be described as "splendorous," moments when the formless takes form and you see the magic of it, then you're grateful and your hope is that this God given beauty may remain with us all forever.

Beauty is nourishment for the human soul. It nourishes that in us which is impalpable, draws us to the invisible which underlies all

that we see. The beauty of nature is a gift created just for us. To preserve the naturalness of our environment, what remains is more important than any change we can bring. The best investment we can make now and for the future is unspoiled land, fruitful land, virgin and potent as it was given to us.

Painting is not depiction only but direct experience, the result of intense observation. It defies the limitations of paint and two-dimensional canvas, transporting one into a timeless, everlasting world, a world not frozen as is an image, but a vibrant, living world, vital and energetic. I am finally realizing that I don't want to paint pictures of things or places, even though I am inspired by them. I want to paint my experience of each one. I want to experience them not as scenes or objects or people, but as mysterious, miraculous, wonderful manifestations of the invisible transformed into the visible."

Sir Roland Richardson

Golden Grove Plantation, Colombier
Original "Plein Air" Oil painted on location from life
by Sir Roland Richardson | 26 inches x 81 inches | June 2014

"Live life with a little spice"

Mains and Sides

Temptation's Filet Mignon

Serves 4

4	Beef tenderloin steaks cut into 8 oz portions
as needed	Olive oil
as needed	Salt and pepper
as desired	Mashed potatoes (see page 180)
as needed	Chimichurri (see page 183)
as needed	Pickled red onions (see page 183)

Season steaks with olive oil, salt and pepper. It is a good idea to take the steaks out of refrigeration 20-30 minutes before grilling as the center will still be very cold if you wish to cook until medium rare.

Grill steaks to your desired doneness. Medium rare is recommended. Let rest 5 minutes.

To plate: Spoon approximately ¾ cup mashed potatoes in the center of a nice round white plate. Place beef tenderloin on top, and finish with chimichurri and pickled red onions.

When you choose to splurge out on a steak, quality is key. Go with top of the line PRIME, but be careful of savvy misleading labels and words like "choice or select" which give the impression of something decadent. To those who don't know, these are the 2nd and 3rd quality grades. We have been very successful with Certified Angus Beef for over a decade.

I don't over do it with garnishes and sauces because I want the steak to be the star... and of the so many recipes for chimichurri, I have yet to find one that I enjoy more than this very simple version. This has been a no. 1 on our menu for years, gaining much fanfare.

Grilled Tuna Steak
with Caribbean Vegetable Slaw and Wasabi Mashed Potatoes

Serves 4

4	Best quality, fresh tuna cut into 6oz portions
as needed	Olive oil
as needed	Salt and pepper
as needed	Asian grilling glaze (see page 179)
as needed	Black and white sesame seeds
1 tsp	Wasabi
3 cups	Mashed potatoes (see page 180)

The possibilities with tuna are endless...from seared to cold and salads too. I like to approach tuna as if it were a steak, and therefore, I present it with mash, similar to our Filet Mignon. We even use the chimichurri as one of the components for the salad dressing. This is a simple easy dish that will get you a lot of kudos from your foodie friends.

Season the tuna steaks with olive oil, salt and pepper. Crust with sesame seeds. Place on grill and cook to your desired "doneness" (medium rare is highly recommended). Brush with Asian grilling glaze and allow the sauce to caramelize a bit on the grill. Set tuna aside to rest for 3-5 minutes.

In the meantime, stir the wasabi into the mash potatoes and heat (in microwave or oven).

Caribbean Vegetable Slaw

½ cup	Green papaya (julienned)
½	Granny Smith apple (julienned)
½ cup	Fresh fennel (julienned)
½ cup	Christophine (julienned)
½ cup	Pumpkin (julienned)
2 tbs	Pickled red onions (see page 183)
2 tbs	Chimichurri (see page 183)

In a bowl, combine all ingredients and set aside until ready to use.

To plate: Place an approximately ¾ cup mound of mashed potatoes in the center of a large white round plate. Put grilled tuna on top and finish with roughly ½ cup of Caribbean Vegetable Slaw. Garnish with some sesame seeds and cilantro, or mint.

This dish is a sure hit when you are craving "Chinese take-out". Nobody does duck better than the Chinese. This technique of frying and then coating the duck with a rich glaze will give you a delightful soft-crispy texture as the crispy fried duck absorbs the moisture from the sauce. Be sure to save the duck skins for rendering into duck fat... for chefs this is like liquid gold.

Asian Vegetable Basmati Stir Fried

1 tsp	GGS (ginger, garlic, scallion)
1 tsp	Olive oil
2 tsps	Sesame oil
¼ cup	Celery (finely chopped)
¼ cup	Carrots (finely chopped)
¼ cup	Mushrooms (sliced)
¼ cup	Red bell pepper (finely chopped)
½ cup	Fresh basil leaves
½ cup	Baby bok choy (roughly chopped)
2 tbs	Ketchap Manis
2 tbs	Chicken broth
3 cups	Pre-cooked basmati rice

In a sauté pan or wok, over a high heat, quickly stir fry GGS with olive oil and sesame oil. Add vegetables, Ketchap Manis and chicken broth. Stir fry until vegetables have been cooked, but are still crispy. Add rice and continue to mix until all combined.

To plate: On a rectangular plate, spoon the rice in a long neat row. Lay the duck breast pieces neatly on top of the rice. Garnish with daikon cress, sesame seeds and fresh cilantro.

Shrimp and Chicken Pad Thai
with Coconut Curried Rice Noodles and Asian-Veggie Stir Fry

This is definitely not authentic ... but seriously unless you're in Thailand, eating on the street, you won't have authentic Pad Thai, period. Plus authentic doesn't always mean better. This is one of my personal favorite dishes on the menu, and it is usually what I choose on the rare nights I am lucky enough to be eating dinner, as a guest, in my own restaurant.

Serves 4

4	Chicken breasts (skin on) approx. 5ozs each
8	Jumbo shrimp 8-12 size
as needed	Olive oil
as needed	Salt and pepper
as needed	Asian glaze (see page 179)
3 cups	Rice noodles (cooked) *
2 cups	Pad Thai sauce (see page 179)
½ cup	Carrots (julienned)
½ cup	Shiitake mushrooms (sliced)
1 head	Baby bok choy (rough chopped)
1 bunch	Fresh basil (leaves separated)
4 sprigs	Cilantro or micro cilantro (for garnish)
1 tsp	Black and white sesame seeds (for garnish)
1 tbs	Soy-balsamic syrup (see page 186)
as needed	Crushed toasted peanuts

Season chicken and shrimp with olive oil, salt and pepper. Place on grill (skin side down first) and grill until both the chicken and shrimp are fully cooked. Be careful, the shrimp will cook faster than the chicken breast. While grilling, brush liberally with the Asian grilling glaze.

Meanwhile in a large sauté pan, over high heat, add the Pad Thai sauce, vegetables and basil leaves. Simmer for 3-4 minutes until vegetables are cooked, but still have some crunch. Add rice noodles and continue to cook until the sauce is absorbed.

To plate: Using a ring mold place about 1 cup of noodles on a plate, trying to keep as neat and centered as possible. Place a chicken breast on the noodles and two shrimps on top of the chicken. Garnish with a cilantro sprig, sesame seeds, crushed toasted peanuts and balsamic-soy syrup.

* To cook rice noodles. Place rice noodles in a large enough container. Add boiling water to the container, and let it sit for approximately 10 minutes. Strain off the water and keep the cooked al dente noodles until ready to use.

Red Wine Braised Veal Osso Bucco
with Roasted Peppers and Mushroom Risotto

Serves 4

4	Veal shanks
1 sprig	Fresh rosemary
as needed	Chicken broth
as needed	Osso bucco braising sauce (see page 177)
1	Roasted red pepper, roughly chopped
2 cups	Mushrooms, rough chopped
2 tbs	Truffle butter (see page 181)
¼ cup	Heavy cream

Place veal shanks and rosemary sprig in a deep baking pan and add enough chicken stock to cover the veal shanks. Tightly cover with foil and place into a 300°F oven for 2 hours. Once cooked, remove shanks from broth and set aside until ready to use. (Save the cooking liquid for risotto. You will have an enriched chicken-veal stock. It is delicious for cooking beans, rice or pasta as well).

Place the par-cooked veal shanks in a medium saucepan and cover with the osso bucco braising sauce, roasted red peppers and mushrooms. Simmer for 15-20 minutes, or until the veal shank has been heated through and flavors are absorbed. Remove veal shank and hold warm, allowing sauce to lightly reduce to a thickened consistency. Enrich the braising sauce with truffle butter and heavy cream. The sauce will thicken as it reduces.

Mushroom Risotto

as needed	Olive oil
½	Onion (minced)
1½ cup	Arborio rice
4 cups	Enriched chicken-veal broth from par cooking veal shanks
1 cup	Mushroom sauce (see page 178)
½ cup	Parmgiano Reggiano (freshly grated)
as needed	Micro basil (for garnish)

In a sauté pan, over a medium heat, add olive oil and sauté the onion. Add Arborio rice and continue to sauté for one minute. Add one cup of the broth reserved from cooking the veal shanks. Continue to stir the rice until it absorbs all the liquid. Add one more cup, and repeat this step two more times. The risotto should now be cooked 70-80%. Set aside until ready to use.

To finish the risotto, heat one cup of mushroom sauce in a saucepan, add three cups of the pre-cooked risotto and the freshly grated Parmgiano cheese. Continue to stir until the risotto is creamy and has absorbed the flavors of the mushroom sauce.

To plate: Place about ¾ cups mushroom risotto on the plate and top with the osso bucco. Don't worry if the meat falls apart, this is actually a good thing. Spoon generously with the braising sauce, and garnish with some micro basil.

We have not taken this dish off the menu in our 10 years. This is "gourmet comfort" at its best. Roasted peppers and mushrooms add a nice earthy flavor component. This dish is surprisingly easy, but does require patience. "Low and slow" are key here. You can serve this with so many side items... from polenta to mash, or pasta.

Lal, Oneka and Denise
Kitchen Capers

Caramelized Shallot Braised Short Ribs
with Cheddar Polenta and Seasonal Market Vegetables

Serves 4

4	Beef short ribs 10-14oz each (including bone)
as needed	Chicken stock (enough to cover the short ribs)
as needed	Short rib braising sauce (see page 177)
¼ cup	Shallot marmalade (see page 182)
2 tbs	Salted butter (cold, cut in small cubes)

Place short ribs in a deep roasting pan and add enough chicken stock to almost cover them. Tightly cover with foil and place into a 300°F oven for 3-4 hours. Once cooked, remove the short ribs from pan and save enriched chicken broth for making a soup, cooking dirty rice or beans.

Place the par-cooked short ribs in a medium saucepan and add short rib braising sauce and shallot marmalade. Simmer for 20 minutes, or until the short ribs have absorbed the flavors of the new sauce. Remove the short ribs and keep warm. Allow sauce to lightly reduce to a thickened consistency, and enrich by whisking in butter.

Market Vegetables

2 cups	Mixed seasonal vegetables, such as zucchini, fennel, carrots, peppers (diced)
as needed	Olive oil
as needed	Salt and pepper

Sauté vegetables over high heat with the olive oil. Add few drops of water or chicken broth to help pan-steam the vegetables. Finish by seasoning the vegetables with salt and pepper.

4 ozs	Butter
1 cup	Grated cheddar cheese
as needed	Salt and pepper

In a medium sauce pan, bring water to boil. Whisk in corn meal. Let polenta cook over low heat, while stirring until corn meal is fully cooked (approximately 20 minutes). Fold in cream cheese, heavy cream, butter, and grated cheese. Adjust seasoning with salt, and pepper

To plate: Place approximately 1 cup of cheddar polenta in the center of a shallow bowl . Place short rib on top. It doesn't matter if meat falls off bone. Just place back on bone. Cover the short rib generously with shallot sauce. Neatly arrange vegetables around the short rib. Garnish with chopped chives.

In Temptation, I often stand by the garbage bin looking at the plates coming back. I'm looking to see how much of the food actually gets eaten, or whether in fact anything comes back ... and whether it is a side item or the main item ... this science, affectionately known as " garbology ", helps me to tweak!! With flavors or portion sizes to ultimately get the winning formula. And, just to let you know, these short ribs need no tweaking, this plate ALWAYS come back clean, almost licked. Making it a very easy job for the dishwasher.

"Many people cry when chopping onions, the trick is not to form an emotional bond"

Eggplant-Portabello Crusted Salmon Fillet
with Clams, Italian Sausage, Garlicky Fish Broth and Purple Mash

Serves 4

4	Salmon fillets (6-8ozs each) (fresh)
as needed	Olive oil, salt and pepper
4 tbs	Eggplant hummus (see page 27)
1	Portabello mushroom
¼ cup	Balsamic vinaigrette (see page 181)
3 cups	Purple mashed potato (see page 180)
1 cup	Fish broth
1 cup	Clam juice
½ cup	Fresh dill and tarragon (chopped)
4 ozs	Garlic butter, (cold cut in cubes) (see page 181)
4 ozs	Italian sausage
12	Cherry stone clams

This is called a poor man's "surf 'n turf". While there are several components to this dish, I promise you that you will impress anyone who you prepare this for. How can you go wrong with the combination of eggplant, portabello mushrooms, sausage, clams and garlic? If you don't have salmon or mash potatoes, these ingredients will also make a delicious pasta.

Pre-heat oven to 375°F. Season salmon fillets with olive oil, salt and pepper. In a hot sauté pan, sear the bottom side of the salmon for one minute.

Spread the eggplant hummus on the top side of the salmon (the side that is not seared). Marinate portabello mushroom in balsamic vinaigrette for 10-15 minutes, and grill until fully cooked. Slice the grilled portabello in small pieces and neatly place slices on top of the eggplant hummus crusted salmon. Place the salmon in the oven for 5-7 minutes to finish cooking.

Make sure your mashed potatoes are heated up, either in the microwave or oven. Bring the fish broth and clam juice to boil. Add the chopped dill and tarragon, and whisk in the garlic butter to enrich the sauce. Finally add the Italian sausage and clams to mixture and simmer until clams open and Italian sausage is fully cooked. (3-4 mintues).

To plate: Place a mound of mashed potato in the center of a shallow 12 inch bowl/plate with the salmon fillet on top. Spoon the clam and sausage mixture around the potatoes and garnish with more tarragon, and dill.

93

Whole Market Fish (for two)
with Coconut Rice, Stir Fried Asian Vegetables and Citrus Glaze

Serves 2

1½ – 2lbs	Fresh whole fish (scaled and gutted)
as needed	Olive oil
as needed	Salt and pepper
1 cup	Rice flour
¾ cup	Club soda (cold)
½ cup	Citrus glaze (see page 179)

Pre-heat the frying oil to 350°F. Pat fish dry with paper towels. Season fish with olive oil, salt and pepper. Prepare the tempura batter with rice flour and club soda. The batter should resemble the consistency of a crepe or thin pancake batter. Deep fry the fish for 6-8 minutes. Let fish rest on paper towels for two minutes. Brush fish with citrus glaze.

Coconut Rice

2 cups | Basmati rice (cooked)
½ cup | Coconut milk
½ cup | Scallions (sliced thin)
¼ cup | Sliced almonds (toasted)
as needed | Salt and pepper

In a small saucepan, over medium heat, add rice, coconut milk, scallions and almonds. Heat until warmed through and adjust seasoning.

Stir Fried Asian Vegetables

1 tbs | Sesame oil
1 tbs | Basil oil (see page 180)
1 tsp | Ginger (minced)
½ cup | Carrots (julienned)
½ cup | Mushrooms (sliced)

½ cup | Red bell peppers (julienned)
1 cup | Baby bok choy (sliced)
10 spears | Asparagus (blanched)
¼ cup | Chicken broth (see page 187)
as needed | Salt and pepper

In a sauté pan, over high heat, add sesame and basil oils. Add ginger and sweat until you can smell the aroma. Then add the rest of the vegetables and chicken broth. Cover with a lid or foil, and let vegetables pan steam for 3-4 minutes. Adjust seasoning and hold until ready to use.

To Plate: On a large platter, place a bed of rice in the center. Rest fish on top of this bed of rice and top with the vegetables. Garnish with black and white sesame seeds, fresh cilantro sprigs, basil oil, and a few drops of soy sauce.

This is always a crowd pleaser. The simple technique of using kitchen scissors to remove the bones, and create a butterfly-like opening on the fish makes for easy eating as well. The coconut rice and stir fried veggies are a great complement for the Asian inspired tempura fish. Seabass, Branzino and Red Snapper work very well for this recipe.

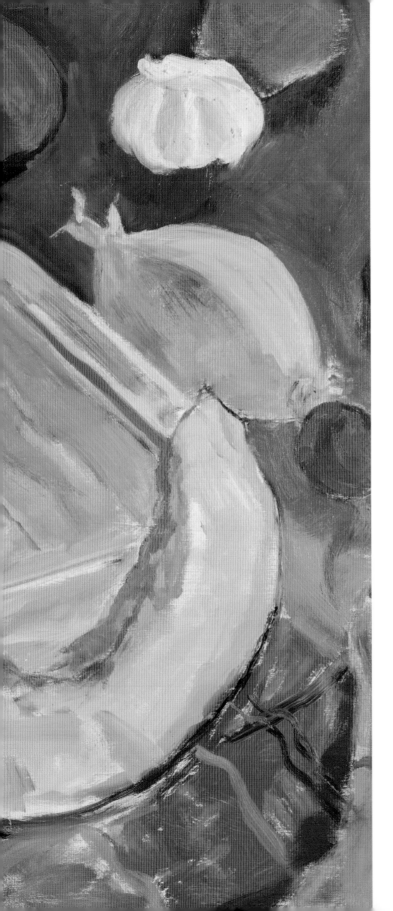

Provisions

What better way to plan to feed
than taking time to plant a seed …
The corn grows tall amidst a field
where okra, beans and tanya yield,
and sweet potatoes spread their vine
while 'neath the soil, roots intertwine.
Pidgeon peas pop when they're done
in cruda bags laid in the sun,
for evening soup or mixed in rice,
so nourishing, so very nice.
The fruits & berries,
grains & veggies
all start with just one need,
their chance to grow, to multiply,
begins with just one seed.

Poem by Laura Richardson

Pot Fish and Sweet Potatoes

Original Oil painted from life by Sir Roland Richardson
21.5 inches x 32 inches | April 2009

12 strips	Salmon bacon *
as needed	Olive oil
as needed	Salt and pepper

Peel shrimp, but do not remove tips. Save shells for sauce, broth or stock. Split shrimp open, from the top to the bottom on the outer edge. Remove vein and rinse under cold water. Pat shrimp dry.

Make crab stuffing by combining crab, mayonnaise, breadcrumbs, onions, celery, apples, parsley and dill. Stuff cavity of shrimp, from top to bottom with mixture and wrap shrimp with the salmon bacon. Season the shrimp with olive oil, salt and pepper. Place shrimp in a pre-heated oven for 4-5 minutes or until just barely cooked. Shrimp will overcook very quickly, so be careful. Thirty seconds can make a big difference between juicy and dry.

* Salmon bacon is sometimes available in supermarkets. If not, by all means used smoked salmon or regular pork bacon.

½ cup	Heavy cream
2 tbs	Truffle butter or garlic butter (see page 181)
1 cup	Zucchini (julienned)
½ cup	Cherry tomatoes roughly chopped
½ cup	Assorted mushrooms
½ cup	Red bell peppers (julienned)
2 cups	Israeli couscous (cooked as you would cook pasta)
½ cup	Grated Parmigiano Reggiano cheese
1 tbs	Lemon zest
1 tbs	Fresh basil

In a sauté pan, bring the stock, heavy cream and butter to a simmer. Add vegetables and let them cook for 2-3 minutes. Add pasta, grated cheese and lemon zest.

To Plate: On a rectangular plate, place pasta in a neat line along the center of the plate. Place the three shrimps in a row with tails sticking up. Garnish with your favorite herbs, like fresh oregano, micro basil and chives.

Sometimes, even I amaze myself... this is one of those dishes I should have come up with 10 years ago. I tasted salmon bacon at a food show and promised myself that I would make a dish utilizing this product. It has only been on our menu for a couple months, and it is one of those dishes that our wait staff enjoy recommending when a guest seems stumped making a choice.

"Happiness is knowing there's a cake in the oven"

Serves 4

Saffron Rice

2 cups	Basmati rice
as needed	Olive oil
4 cups	Shellfish broth (see page 186)
1 tsp	Saffron threads

In a saucepan, sauté basmati rice with olive oil. Add the shellfish broth and saffron. Stir until broth reaches a boil. Lower the fire and cover pot with a lid or foil and let the rice simmer for 18-20 minutes. This rice can be made up to three days ahead.

Lobster Tails

as needed	Olive oil
1 tsp	Garlic (minced)
4	Lobster tails (cut into bite size pieces, reserve the tails/shells)
2 ozs	Cognac
½ cup	Heavy cream
as needed	Salt and pepper

In a sauté pan, over high heat, add olive oil and garlic. After the flavor of the garlic has been released, add the lobster and continue to cook until almost done. Deglaze the pan with cognac, and add heavy cream. Season to taste with salt and pepper. Blanch the empty shells for one minute until bright red. Fill the lobster back into the warm, empty shells for the presentation.

Corn Broth

1 cup	Fresh or frozen corn kernels
2 cups	Shellfish or chicken broth (see page 187)
1 tbs	Butter
½ tsp	Cumin
as needed	Salt, pepper and sugar

In a saucepan, bring corn, broth, butter and cumin to a boil. Make sure the corn is cooked if using fresh kernels. Pour mixture into a blender to puree. Strain and set aside until ready to use.

Assembling "The Paella"

as needed	Olive oil
12	Clams
4	Mussels
½ cup	Sliced chorizo (mild or hot)
½ cup	Green peas
2 cups	Corn broth

In a sauté pan on high heat, add olive oil, clams, mussels and chorizo. Saute for 2-3 minutes, add peas and corn broth. Cook until the mussels and clams open up. Add basmati rice and mix until everything is heated through. The rice will absorb the corn broth and is ready when it has a delicious, moist appearance. Place lobster tails in a decorative pattern on top of the rice and serve, family style, in the same sauté pan.

We make a delicious shellfish broth using clam juice, saffron, shrimp shells and lobster heads. Using a corn puree adds a dimension of sweetness that matches the shellfish, and is magical with the chorizo. This is a great special occasion feast for New Year's Eve or Valentine's etc.

"Fish 'n Chips" Potato Crusted Branzino Fillet

with Celery Root Purée, Truffle Buerre Blanc, Chanterelles and Salmon Roe

Serves 4

4	Branzino fillets (5 oz each)
as needed	Olive oil
as needed	Salt and pepper
2	Potatoes

Season branzino fillets with olive oil, salt and pepper. Cut potatoes into a spiral using a Japanese slicer. You want to create a long strands of potato.

Wrap each fish fillet in the strands of potato as if you were wrapping a piece of string around a stick. Set aside until ready to use. Just before being ready to serve, deep fry the potato wrapped fish for two minutes or until the potatoes have become golden brown and crispy.

Depending on the size of the fillets, you may need to finish the fish in a low 275°F oven for no more than 3-5 minutes.

Celery Root Purée

2 cups	Celery root
	(peeled, and rougly chopped)
½ cup	Heavy cream
2 tbs	Butter
as needed	Salt and pepper

In a large pot bring celery root to a boil in water. Cook until celery root is fork tender. Drain and place celery root in a mixing bowl. Add cream, butter and seasonings. Follow the same procedure as you would for mashed potato.

Truffle Beurre Blanc

2 ozs	White wine
1 tbs	Shallots minced
2 ozs	Heavy cream
1 cup	Truffle butter, cubed (see page 181)
1 cup	Chanterelles

In a saucepan, over high heat, add white wine, shallots and heavy cream. Bring to simmer and let reduce by half. Reduce heat to low and, with a whisk, start adding the cubes of butter to the reduction, whisk until melted. Continue until butter is incorporated. Finally add chanterelles and keep sauce warm. Adjust seasoning with salt and pepper. Prepare sauce at least 30 minutes before being ready to use so that the chanterelles have time to absorb the flavors of the sauce and cook a little bit.

Garnishes

4 tsps	Salmon roe
as needed	Fresh herbs such as dill, chives, tarragon

To plate: Place some celery root purée in the center of a plate. Top with the fish and spoon sauce around the plate, scattering the chanterelles. Garnish the top of fish with salmon roe, and herbs.

"This is how I roll"

Seared Scallops
with Spaghetti Squash "Carbonara"

Serves 4

12 | Jumbo scallops (U15)
as needed | Salt and pepper
as needed | Olive oil

Pat scallops dry, and season with salt and pepper. In a non stick sauté pan, over high heat, add olive oil. When the oil is hot, add scallops and sear. (Scallops have a high sugar content, and when seared properly they get nicely caramelized. This is part of the appeal of a great scallop dish).

After two minutes, turn scallops over and continue to cook over high heat on the other side. If scallops are not fully cooked, place them in a low 250°F oven for a few minutes until fully cooked.

Spaghetti Squash

1 | Spaghetti squash
as needed | Olive oil

Pre-heat oven to 350°F. Cut spaghetti squash in half (length wise). Place upside down in a roasting pan and add just enough water so that you have a thin layer at the bottom of the pan. Cover with foil and roast squash until fully cooked. (Approx. 30 minutes).

After squash is roasted, let cool completely, then scrape out the flesh with a fork. It will come out in thin strands that resemble spaghetti. This will be your "pasta" for the dish.

Carbonara Sauce

as needed	Olive oil
4 strips	Bacon (minced)
1 clove	Garlic (minced)
1 cup	Green peas
2 cups	Heavy cream
½ cup	Parmigiano Reggiano
as needed	Salt and pepper
2 tsps	Salmon roe (for garnish)
as needed	Fresh tarragon or chives (for garnish)

In a sauté pan, over high heat, add bacon and let it render. Add garlic and green peas. Remove some of the fat and save it for another use. Add cream and bring it up to a simmer. Add spaghetti squash and heat until everything is heated through. Add Parmigiano Reggiano and toss until all is combined. Adjust seasoning with salt and pepper

To plate: Place the "pasta" in a nice pasta bowl or on a long rectangular plate, and neatly place three scallops per plate. Garnish with salmon roe, fresh tarragon and chives.

Shellfish and bacon are a no brainer. Bacon wrapped scallops have been done by so many for so long. Here, we use bacon in carbonara sauce along with peas and parmigiano to create a newer lighter version of a scallops and pasta dish. Try to source dry, (i.e. never frozen) scallops as they will caramelize nicely and not shrink.

"It started with a kiss ..."

(special order at your supermarket or butcher)

as needed | Salt, pepper and olive oil

1 cup | Shallot reduction (see page 124)

When grilling, it is always best to remove the steaks from refrigeration 20-30 minutes before cooking so that the center will not be cold if you like your steaks medium rare. Rub the steaks with salt, pepper and olive oil. Place on the grill and cook until your desired doneness. For this steak I recommend 6-8 minutes per side for medium.

Potato Churros

Experienced cooks will know that this is just pâte à choux with cooked potatoes folded in.

1 cup | Water

1 stick | Butter

1 cup | Flour

1 cup | Eggs (approximately 4-6 eggs)

2 cups | Potatoes (boiled and mashed)

as needed | Salt, pepper

as needed | Oil for deep frying pre-heated to 350°F

Bring water and butter to boil. Once butter has melted, stir in flour and, with a wooden spoon, mix vigorously until the mixture pulls away from the sides and forms a ball. Transfer this batter to a stand or hand mixer, and mix on high speed until slightly warm to the touch (approximately 2-3 minutes). Add eggs, one at at a time, and continue to mix until thoroughly combined. Add potato puree and continue to mix until all is combined. Batter should resemble a heavy mash potato. Place this batter in a pastry bag fitted with a star tip, and pipe 4-6 inch long "churros" into the hot oil to fry. Fry them until gold brown and crispy. Drain on paper towel. You can make these ahead and keep them warm.

Cognac Glazed Mushrooms

1 tbs	Garlic butter (see page 181)
1 tbs	EVOO
2 cups	Mushrooms (finely chopped)
2 oz	Cognac
2 oz	Heavy cream
2 tsp	Freshly chopped chives
as needed	Salt and pepper

In a sauté pan, over medium to high heat, add garlic butter and EVOO. Once butter has melted, add mushrooms and sauté until the mushrooms are fully cooked, and almost dry. Deglaze with cognac, be careful as the pan will flambé. Add the heavy cream, chives and season with salt, and pepper.

To Plate: Spoon a little bit of shallot reduction in the center of a large round white plate. Place the grilled steak on top of the sauce. Top with mushrooms and garnish with potato churros.

If you are a steak lover then this dish will knock your socks off. The Wagyu or Kobe style flat iron is "hands down" the cut of steak that combines the best of flavor and texture for a great steak eating experience. A seriously beefy flavor, combined with melt in your mouth tenderness. As with any premium steak, let the sauces and garnishes just serve as a complement and let the star of the dish be the steak.

"Sabroso"

Mc Dino's Burger

Kobe Burger with Heirloom Tomato, Organic Greens, Mac 'n Cheese and "Secret Sauce"

Serves 4

2 lbs	Kobe ground beef (good quality 80/20 ground beef is also a great substitute)
as needed	Salt and pepper
as needed	"Secret Sauce"
1 portion	Mac 'n Cheese (see page 120)
½ cup	Grated mix cheeses (cheddar, Gouda, Swiss, mozzarella)
¼ cup	Organic mixed field greens
1	Kumato (sliced)

Pre-heat your grill to high and your oven to 400° F. Season the Kobe ground beef with salt and pepper. Form them into 8oz burger patties. A great trick is to use an empty tuna fish can that has been opened on both sides.

Place the burger patties on the grill to sear on both sides. Top each patty with Mac 'n Cheese and grated cheese. Place the patties in the oven and cook for 5-8 minutes for a medium burger.

To assemble: Place "Secret Sauce" generously on both sides of the bun. Place lettuce and tomato on the top side of the bun. Place the patty with Mac 'n Cheese on the bottom side of the bun, and serve with your favorite side dish.

My love for burgers will never die. Being surrounded everyday with gourmet food, and ingredients from morel mushrooms to smoked duck can be overwhelming. Even in culinary school, an escape to a local diner for a juicy burger was always such a treat.

We change our burger often, and I encourage you to do the same. Some other ideas for toppings would be seared foie gras, sautéed mushrooms, fried egg, potato chips and even pulled pork.

Secret Sauce

1/3 cup each	Mayonnaise, mustard, ketchup and hot dog relish
5 drops	Tabasco

Mix all ingredients in and use as needed.

Rack of Lamb
with Spinach-Lentil Risotto and Butternut Squash Curry
Serves 4

2	Full racks of lamb (Frenched) (we use New Zealand spring lamb)
as needed	Olive oil, salt and pepper

Pre-heat grill to high. Cut lamb into single or double bone portions. In a full rack there are 8 bones. Season the rack of lamb with olive oil, salt and pepper. Place on the grill and cooked on both sides to your desired doneness. For medium rare 4-5 minutes per side is enough.

Spinach Lentil Risotto

as needed	Olive oil	cup	Puy lentils (cooked)
½	Onion (small diced)	1 cup	Spinach (finely chopped)
2 cups	Arborio rice	cup	Freshly grated Parmigiano cheese
¼ cup	White wine	cup	Heavy cream
6 cups	Chicken broth	as needed	Salt and pepper

In a saucepan, over medium high heat, add olive oil and sauté the onion just until it starts to sweat. Add the Arborio rice and sauté the rice until it is combined with the onion. Add the wine, and stir the risotto constantly until the wine is reduced by half. Add one third of the chicken broth and continue to stir until most of the broth has been absorbed. Add another third of the broth, and repeat stirring until it has been absorbed. Add the last third and repeat until it is absorbed. This should take 20-30 minutes if done correctly. Before plating, fold in cooked lentils, spinach, Parmigiano and a little heavy cream, and adjust the seasoning.

Butternut Squash Curry

1 cup	Coconut curry sauce (see page 184)
¼ cup	Butternut squash purée (see page 121) (same as pumpkin purée)
1 tsp	Chimichurri sauce (see page 183)

In a saucepan over medium high heat, combine the curry sauce and squash purée. Whisk until the purée is fully incorporated in the sauce. Bring to a simmer and add chimichurri sauce

To plate: Using a small ring mold, make a nice round mold of the risotto on the plate. Lean the chops against the risotto and spoon sauce around the plate.

This dish is a personal favorite of mine. New Zealand lamb chops have a mild flavor and are super tender. The butternut squash curry sauce is a great example of having fun and experimenting in the kitchen with "mise en place". It is a great way to discover new, creative ways to cross utilize menu items.

Mac 'n' Cheese Three Ways
Traditional, Pumpkin and Spinach

Serves 4

16 oz	Elbow macaroni, shells, or penne (cooked)
3½ cups	Cheese sauce (see page 122)
¼ cup	Grated Swiss cheese
¼ cup	Grated Gouda cheese
¼ cup	Grated mozzarella
¼ cup	Grated cheddar cheese

Pre-heat oven to 400°F. In a saucepan, bring cheese sauce to a gentle simmer, add in the cooked pasta and stir until coated. Transfer to a baking dish (at the restaurant we use individual baking dishes) and top with grated cheeses and bake for approximately 8 minutes or until the cheese on top is golden brown and bubbly. Serve hot!

Pumpkin Mac 'n' Cheese

Pumpkin Purée

1	Pumpkin (peeled and diced)
½ cup	Milk
2 oz	Butter
as needed	Salt, pepper and nutmeg

Make pumpkin purée as you would make mash potatoes. Cook the pumpkin and purée with the milk, butter and seasonings. Enjoy as is, or fold into the mac 'n' cheese by only using two cups of cheese sauce and adding one cup of pumpkin purée to the saucepan before adding the pasta. Top with grated cheeses and crushed tortilla chips.

Spinach Mac 'n' Cheese

Spinach Purée

10 oz	Fresh spinach (blanched and shocked)
2 tbs	Water
as needed	Salt and pepper

Combine blanched and cooled spinach in blender with the water. Purée until it resembles a thick purée, like a smoothie. Adjust seasoning with salt and pepper. Fold this spinach purée into the cheese sauce, and proceed to prepare the mac 'n' cheese as previously mentioned.

Cheese Sauce

1 cup	Cream cheese
1 cup	Cheese whiz
2 cup	Heavy cream

In a sauce pan over medium heat, combine the cream cheese, cheese whiz and heavy cream until all is melted.

Like our onion soup, this has become one of those "must order" items when visiting Temptation. This dish is so addictive it has often been called "Crack 'n cheese" by loyal supporters. Besides the three variations above, there are an endless array of possible add-ins that would be delicious with mac 'n' cheese. Some of my suggestions are mushrooms, bacon, crab, lobster, peppers, tomatoes, peas, Tabasco, corn, chorizo, ham, BBQ chicken, arugula, shrimp or even pumpkin from the "Woman Under a Tree".

The lovely Olive | Marigot Market

Woman Under a Tree

Imagine making a living,
under a tree,
trading her fruit
for passers' money.

Stacking her mangoes,
ripening fast by the sun,
hoping they're sold
by the time the day's done.

Cars slow, then they turn,
to just drive away,
when throughout that long moment
she stands still to pray.

Pumpkins, papayas,
and plantains remain,
while strangers decide
on her loss or her gain.

I did that one morning,
when passing her by.
She waited with patience
then let out a sigh.

The next time I see her,
I'll buy that pumpkin.
Though short on a recipe,
she'll know where to begin.

Poem by Laura Richardson

Clairsina
Fine Art Limited Edition
from an Original Oil
painted from life
by Sir Roland Richardson

Creamed Spinach

Serves 6-8

20 oz	Fresh spinach (two packets finely chopped)
2 cups	Heavy cream
1 tsp	Shallot (minced)
1 tsp	Garlic (minced)
1 cup	Mozzarella (grated)
½ cup	Parmigiano (grated)
½ cup	Panko bread crumbs
½ cup	Cream cheese (cut in small cubes)
as needed	Salt, pepper and nutmeg
as needed	Olive oil

Combine half of the spinach and half heavy cream in a pot. Cook until spinach has completely wilted. This will only take 2 minutes as the spinach cooks down very quickly. Purée mixture in blender and set aside to cool.

In a sauté pan, add olive oil and sauté shallots and garlic. Add remaining spinach, heavy cream, mozzarella and Parmigiano. Just cook until spinach is wilted again, not more than 2-3 minutes. Adjust seasoning with salt, pepper and nutmeg. Set aside to cool.

In a mixing bowl, combine spinach puree with the spinach-cheese mixture. Fill resulting mixture into ramekins and top with Panko and cream cheese. Bake in a 375F oven for 5-7 minutes until the top has melted and browned nicely.

This is probably the most popular side order in steak houses. I personally love this, because it satisfies the guilty pleasure of having a rich, creamy, cheesy dish while still knowing I've had my serving of vegetables for the day. If you're daring, spice this up with cumin and coriander for an Indian spin. This is easy to prepare and can be made ahead of time.

Roasted Beets 'n' Goat Cheese
Serve as a main or a side

Serves 4

2	Beets (peeled)
½ cup	White Balsamic vinegar
2 cups	Water
as needed	Crumbled goat cheese
as needed	Pine nuts
as needed	Arugula
as needed	EVOO
as needed	Salt and pepper

Bring beets to boil with balsamic vinegar and water until fork tender. Let cool. Cut into ¼ inch slices. Top with goat cheese and pine nuts. Bake in oven until cheese has melted. Dress arugula leaves with salt, pepper and EVOO (Extra virgin olive oil). Serve beets on top of the arugula.

Beets with goat cheese are becoming the new favorite salad in many restaurants; like the tomato-mozzarella salads of the 90s that were all the rage. This is one of those side orders that we encourage our vegetarian guests to try as this can be a meal by itself.

"Anyone can cook, but only the fearless can be great" *Ratatouille, the movie*

Caribbean Spiced "Ratatouille"
Serve as a main or a side

Serves 4

2 ozs	Olive oil
1 cup	Sweet potato (small diced)
½ cup	Red onion (small diced)
1 tsp	Fresh ginger (minced)
½ cup	Red bell pepper (small diced)
1 cup	Zucchini (small diced)
½ cup	Cherry tomato (cut in quarters)
1 ear	Corn (shucked)
½ cup	Curry sauce (see page 184)
1 tbs	Fresh cilantro
as needed	Salt and pepper

In a pot, sauté sweet potatoes with olive oil and few drops of water so the potatoes pan steam. Continue to sauté for approximately 5 minutes until potatoes are about half-way cooked. Add onions, ginger and bell peppers. Continue to sauté until vegetables have sweated nicely, (do not caramelize). Add zucchini, tomatoes and half of the shucked corn. Continue to sauté until flavors are released. Purée remaining corn kernels with curry sauce in a blender. Add this mixture to vegetables and continue to cook for 5-7 minutes until all ingredients come together. Garnish with fresh cilantro and season with salt and pepper.

This is a great side order for a piece of fish. If you so wish, feel free to add bacon or another smoked ham for a yummy punch of salt to counteract the sweetness of the potatoes and corn.

Sweet Seduction

Sweet, succulent seduction
born from summer's breast,

reaching down like rainbow beads,
bearing Heaven's best.

Swollen seeds surrendering
their pungent, rare perfume,

cords of life, umbilically
grow long beneath green plumes.

Tropical temptations tease
Eve as Adam falls.

Young boys with buckets scramble
uninvited top stone walls.

Lovers lured by lustrous milk,
red nipples ripe to flow,

taunted, hungry hearts await,
mouth-watering mangoes!

Poem by Laura Richardson

Mangoes Ripening in the Sun
Original "Plein Air" Oil painted on location from life by Sir Roland Richardson
27 inches x 30 inches | August 2013

Desserts

Chocolate Cobbler
with Hazelnut Ice Cream and Chocolate Pop Rocks

Serves 4

Chocolate Cake

8 oz	Unsweetened chocolate		1 cup	Buttermilk
2 cups	Coffee		3 cups	All purpose flour
1 cup	Butter (melted)		3 tsps	Baking soda
4 cups	Sugar		1 tsp	Baking powder
9	Eggs		pinch	Salt

Pre-heat oven to 350°F. Melt chocolate and butter in microwave. Add coffee and sugar. Mix until all ingredients have been well combined. Add eggs and buttermilk to chocolate mix and stir until well combined. Do not over mix. Then add all dry ingredients and pour into a greased and floured 13" x 9" cake pan. Bake for 40-50 minutes or until almost set. Cake will continue to cook after it is taken from the oven.

Cobblers (for assembly)

3 cups	Chocolate cake (you can use your favorite recipe as well, but no frosting)
2 cups	Chocolate ganache (see page 182)
as needed	Creusli or crunchy muesli cereal or any combo of chopped nuts and cereal
as needed	Chocolate pop rocks *

In a ramekin, add approx. ½ cup of broken chocolate cake chunks and top with ½ cup chocolate ganache. Top with cereal mixture and place in the oven for five minutes, until heated through. Top with ice cream and pop rocks. Serve immediately.

* Chocolate pop rocks are available online.

Now that this recipe is out, I may have the food police after me wanting to lock me up. Why? This dessert is so amazingly simple, yet so devilishly decadent and delicious, that it should be a crime. Use your favorite ice cream and chocolate cake recipe. The cake recipe we use is actually one from one of the island's legendary bakers Su Wathey from Taloula Mango's restaurant.

Chocolate lends itself to so many combination of flavors, so please have fun with this dessert. If you are a real chocoholic, go with chocolate ice cream, or maybe banana ice cream. Pistachio, coconut or classic vanilla all will work great. This dessert is really about showcasing the delectability of chocolate, and no matter how you top this off, the chocolate will always be the star.

"Mc Dino's" Apple Pie

Serves 4

as needed	Oil for deep frying (either in a pot or table top deep fryer)
3	Granny Smith Apples (peeled, cored and sliced into rings)
1 cup	Rice flour
¾ cup	Ginger ale
as needed	Powdered sugar
as needed	Cinnamon sugar (8 parts sugar, 1 part cinnamon)
as needed	Caramelized walnuts, chopped (see page 182)
as needed	Caramel sauce (see page 183)
as needed	Vanilla ice cream
as needed	Fresh thyme

Prepare oil for frying to 350°F. Slice apples into rings approx. ½ inch thick. Each apple should yield 4-5 slices. Prepare batter with rice flour and ginger ale. Adjust as needed. Batter should look like a tempura or crepe batter.

Dip apples in batter and fry for 2-3 minutes until golden brown and crispy. Immediately toss half the slices in cinnamon sugar, and the other half in powdered sugar.

To plate: Spoon some crushed nuts neatly in one corner of a plate. Place a scoop of ice cream on the chopped nuts. Using a squeeze bottle to make a zigzag of caramel on the base of the plate and then layer the apple slices alternating the two different slices. Sprinkle some freshly picked thyme leaves over the dessert.

An apple dessert is a staple on any dessert menu. Here, we created the flavors of apple pie without actually making a pie. The rice flour batter is simple and makes the apple slices super crispy, which go so well with smooth vanilla and caramel. Add some fresh rosemary to take this to another dimension.

Ricotta Cheesecake
with Amaretto Crust, Pignoli Nuts and "De-constructed"
Rum Raisin Ice Cream

Serves 12

Amaretto Crust

3 cups	Amaretto cookies crushed to powder in food processor
½ stick	Melted butter
pinch	Salt

In a mixing bowl combine ground up cookies, butter and salt.
Mix with a fork and press mixture into a 9-inch spring form pan.

This is my yummy spin on cheesecake. The fun thing about this recipe is that you don't have to follow it. The basic guideline for cheesecake is that for every pound of cheese, you will need 3 eggs to hold it together. After that you add sugar to your desired sweetness and any flavor from chocolate to berries and bananas. You can even use any combo of cheeses from goat to cream and marscapone. This version is an Italian inspiration that always gets rave reviews. Warning you may well get hooked!!!

Cheesecake Filling

1½ lbs	Ricotta cheese	1	Orange (zested)
1 lb	Cream cheese	2 tbs	Vanilla extract
1 cup	Sugar	8	Eggs
2	Lemons (zested)	1 cup	Toasted pignoli nuts

Combine ingredients for filling. Do not over mix. This can be done either in mixing bowl or
with a hand held mixer. Pour into prepared crust and bake for 1-2 hours at 275°F or until set.

"De-constructed" Rum Raisin Ice Cream

1 cup	Dark rum (such as Myers)
2 cups	Raisins
as needed	Vanilla ice cream

Bring rum to a boil, and pour hot rum over the raisins and allow to marcerate for 1 to 2 hours.

To plate: Place some rum soaked raisins in a small cluster on one side of the plate, and place
some vanilla ice cream on top. Place a slice of cheesecake next to this, and drizzle some of
the rum sauce around the plate. Top the cheesecake with some caramelized pine nuts.

Banananana

Banana Bread with Brulee'd Bananas and Banana Ice Cream

Yields 2 loaves

Banana Bread

as needed	Butter for greasing pans
5-6	Very ripe bananas (this is key, about 1½ lbs)
1 tsp	Lemon juice
4 cups	All purpose flour (sifted)
2/3 tsps	Baking powder
2 tsps	Baking soda
pinch	Salt
2 cups	Sugar
2	Eggs (large)
2/3 cup	Vegetable oil
2 cups	Chopped pecans or walnuts

Coat baking pans with butter and pre-heat oven to 350°F. Using a fork, mash bananas with lemon juice. Combine all dry ingredients in a mixing bowl. Add wet ingredients (sugar, eggs, vegetable oil and mashed bananas) to mixture and combine. Fold in nuts and divide equally between baking pans. Bake until center is fully cooked, approx. 45 minutes.

Brulee'd Bananas

1	Banana (sliced into thick slices on a bias)
as needed	Sugar

Arrange slices of banana on a plate or silicone baking sheet. Sprinkle tops with sugar. Using a blow torch, caramelize sugar as you would a crème brulee. Serve immediately.

Ice Cream

See recipe on page 185 or use your favorite store bought ice cream.

To plate: I like to cut a thin slice of banana bread the long way, and arrange the brulee'd bananas and ice cream on top. Drizzle with some chocolate, nuts, caramel and a sprinkling of sea salt.

I don't think there is anyone who doesn't like bananas, or a banana dessert.
If time is an issue, simply do the banana brulée and serve it with ice cream and
some crushed salted peanuts for something whoaaaaa!

This dessert pays tribute to my childhood and to my Indian heritage. In India, it is common to dip Marie biscuits in your tea or Chai. Here, I take that concept to a new level combining the idea of the Latin "Tres Leches" cake.

Cardamom Pound Cake
with Warm Chai (Indian Tres Leches)

Pound Cake

2 sticks	Butter (melted)
6	Eggs (large)
2 2/3 cups	Sugar
3 cups	All purpose flour
½ tsp	Baking soda
½ tsp	Salt
1 cup	Sour cream
1 tbs	Vanilla extract
1 tbs	Cardamom powder

The Chai

1 tbs	Fennel seeds
6	Green cardamom pods
12	Whole cloves
1	Cinnamon stick
½ inch	Fresh ginger, sliced
½ tsp	Black peppercorns
2	Bay leaves
2	Darjeeling tea bags
5 cups	Water
6 tbs	Honey
1 cup	Milk

Pound Cake: Pre-heat oven to 350°F. Grease and flour a baking dish of your choice. (A loaf pan, cup cake molds, bundt pan etc. … it doesn't make a difference).

In a mixing bowl, fitted with paddle attachment, cream together butter, eggs and sugar. Sift and add flour and baking soda. Add salt, sour cream, vanilla and cardamom.

Bake until cake is barely set and a tooth pick comes out still moist. (Cake will continue to cook and set once out of the oven).

The Chai: Bring first nine ingredients to boil, and then turn off heat/fire. Let flavors steep for ten minutes. Strain mixture, add honey and milk.

To plate: In a serving bowl, place some chai on the bottom as a sauce and then place a piece of cake in the center. Sprinkle with a few toasted nuts, like pistachios, almonds or cashews. Dried fruit like apricots can be used around the plate. This is best eaten with a spoon. Let cake soak up the chai.

Coffee 'n Donuts
"Fried to order" Ricotta Donuts with Coffee Ice Cream and Chocolate Ganache

Serves 4 to 6

¼ cup	Sugar
¾ cup	All purpose flour
1 ½ cup	Ricotta cheese
3	Eggs
2 ½ tbs	Baking powder
pinch	Cardamom power
1 cup	Powdered sugar
1 pint	Coffee ice cream (see page 185)
½ cup	Chocolate ganache (see page 182) (warmed)

Pre-heat oil to 350°F. In a mixing bowl combine all ingredients. Let sit outside in a warm area like on top of a warm oven. Using a small ice cream scoop, place small, little 2-oz balls into oil and fry until golden brown and delicious. (Do not worry if they are not perfectly round). Immediately place donuts in a paper bag filled with powdered sugar and shake until they are completely covered.

To plate: Serve on a plate with warm chocolate ganache as a sauce and a scoop of coffee ice cream.

These "fried to order" ricotta donuts are always a hit. This is a simple straightforward batter. I remember the first time I made this, I felt like I was a dessert genius. I use this recipe now when I need to impress a small group of people and don't want to spend all day baking. This can be done start to finish in less than one hour. Pairing them with coffee ice cream or even just a cup of coffee is an obvious match made in powdered sugar heaven.

Flower Pot Dessert

Serves 4

Chocolate Soil

Yields 2 cups or about enough for 4-5 flower pots

2 cups	Chocolate cake crumbs (you can use any chocolate cake recipe or the one we use in our Chocolate Cobbler, see page 136)
½ cup	Chocolate Ganache (see page 182)
1/8 cup	Cinnamon sugar
1/8 cup	Chocolate Pop Rocks (if available, or use chocolate chips)

I must say that this is more of an idea than an actual recipe. My inspiration came from a dining experience at "The Fat Duck" in England where they served their Tiramisu in a clay flower pot. Loving the playful idea of serving a dessert that looks like a whimsical sprouting plant, I decided to adapt this idea for my own restaurant. Just top whatever is buried beneath with some chocolate cake crumbs and garnish with a fresh sprig of mint.

… this is a dessert that always ends up on Facebook, Twitter and Tripadvisor!!!

Here are a few ideas to try in your Flower Pot:

Tiramisu | Mascarpone, whipped cream, espresso, marsala, lady fingers, cocoa powder

Banana Dream Pie | Bananas, pastry cream, caramel ice cream, salted peanuts

Fresh Berry Trifle | Layers of fresh berries, whipped cream, devil's food cake, vanilla ice cream

S'more | Graham Cracker crumbs, marshmallow fluff, chocolate ganache, top with crushed Oreos

Fresh 'n Tropical | Passion fruit mousse, toasted coconut, white chocolate sauce, fresh raspberries and mangoes

Crunchy Chocolate Mousse

Strawberries 'n Cream

White Chocolate, Rasperries and Hazelnut Brittle in layers

Sorbet Trio
Basil, Grapefruit-Honey and Watermelon

Sorbet Base

1 part | Corn syrup
1 part | Simple syrup (equal parts sugar and water)

Basil Sorbet

Yields 1 Quart

5 bunches | Basil (leaves picked)
3 | Lemons (juiced)
1½ cups | Water
2½ cups | Sorbet base

Combine ingredients in a blender. Freeze in an ice cream machine until set (approximately 30 minutes).

Grapefruit-Honey

Yields 1 quart

3 cups | Grapefruit juice (freshly squeezed)
½ cup | Honey
1 cup | Sorbet base

Combine ingredients in a blender. Freeze in an ice cream machine until set.

Watermelon

Yields 1 quart

4 cups | Watermelon (cut into cubes seeds removed)
1 cup | Sorbet base
1 | Lemon (juiced)

Combine ingredients in a blender. Freeze in an ice cream machine until set.

Sorbets are a great refreshing way to end a meal, especially in the warm Caribbean climate. There is a lot of science to sorbet making since all fruits have different levels of water and sugar content. Too much water and your sorbet freezes rock hard. Too much sugar and your sorbet won't freeze. Finding the right balance will require trial and error. You can do an egg test, once your sorbet mixture has been prepared; drop a whole egg into it. If it stays at the bottom, your base has too much sugar. The egg should rise to the top.

We serve our sorbet with a simple garnish, a spring roll wrapper brushed with butter and sprinkled with sugar and salt. It is then toasted until crisp. Feel free to use any tuile, cookie or crepe.

NY Style Cheesecake
with Lychee Sorbet, Fresh Berries and Mint

Serves 12

Amaretto Crust

3 cups | Amaretto cookie crumbs (crushed to powder in a food processor)
½ stick | Butter (melted)
1 pinch | Salt

In a mixing bowl, combine cookie crumbs, butter and salt. Mix with a fork and press this mixture onto the bottom and sides of a 9 inch spring form pan or 12 individual sized spring form pans.

Cheesecake Filling

2½ lbs | Cream cheese (room temperature)
1 cup | Sugar
2 | Lemons zested
1 | Orange zested
2 tbs | Vanilla extract
½ cup | Sour cream
9 | Eggs

Pre-heat oven to 275F. Combine ingredients for the filling, don't over mix. This can be done in a mixing bowl or with a hand-held mixer. Pour into the prepared crust and bake for one and half to two hours, or until the cheesecake is set. Let cool fully and chill. Slice to serve.

Lychee Sorbet

Yield 1 quart

2	|	Cans of lychee (including syrup)
3	|	Limes (juiced and zested)
½ cup	|	Honey
1	|	Egg white

Combine all ingredients in a blender, purée until smooth. Strain the mixture and freeze in an ice cream maker or batch freezer according to the directions. Store in the freezer until ready to use.

To serve: Slice cheesecake and top with a scoop of lychee sorbet and fresh berries. Feel free to substitute the lychee sorbet for one of your favorite flavors.

The fun thing about this recipe is that you don't even have to follow it. The basic guideline for cheesecake is that for every pound of cheese you will need 3 eggs to hold it together. After that, you can add sugar to your desired sweetness and any flavor ... from chocolate to berries, bananas and more. For the crust you can use any cookie you wish, from graham crackers to chocolate cookies, or to amaretto cookies as we use here. You can even use any combo of cheese - from goat to mascarpone. This version is a simple classic NY style cheesecake. I like to use sorbet to contrast the creaminess, and berries to complement the tartness of the cheesecake. Use any flavor you wish.

Chocolate Ganache

... for Truffles

2 parts | Chocolate (roughly chopped)
1 part | Heavy cream

Place chopped chocolate in a clean, dry bowl. Bring heavy cream to boil and pour the cream over the chocolate. Immediately cover the bowl with plastic film for 10-15 minutes. Then gently stir the chocolate and cream mixture until fully melted and combined. Chill in the fridge for 6 hours until set.

To shape the truffles use a melon baller, make small balls from the ganache and roll in your favorite coating – from nuts, to cocoa powder, to coconut flakes and more.

... for Mousse

1 part | Chocolate (roughly chopped)
2 parts | Heavy cream

Prepare the ganache using the same method as above. When the mixture has cooled completely, use a whisk and simply whip the mixture as you would when making whipped cream. Be careful not to over mix.

Two ingredients, with so many possibilities. If you are a chocolate lover, then this simple recipe should be part of your repertoire. Two of the most iconic chocolate treats ever, truffles and mousse can be created with just two simple ingredients. Of course being creative is fun – and with chocolate the possibilities are endless – from liquors to fruits, to nuts and spices, there are so many fun ways to impart your creativity. I would suggest using high quality dark chocolate for these recipes.

157

Payapa, Pineapple and Sea Grapes on Pink Checked Cloth
Original Still Life Oil painted from life
by Sir Roland Richardson
23 inches x 18 inches | April 2009

Waffle French Toast

Serves 4

2 tbs	Butter
1 loaf	Cinnamon raisin bread (unsliced)
2 cups	Milk
6	Egg yolks
½ cup	Sugar
1 tbs	Vanilla extract (or any flavour you wish)
as needed	Maple syrup, honey or agave syrup

Pre-heat waffle iron and brush with butter. Cut bread into 2-inch slices.

Combine milk, egg yolks, sugar and vanilla extract in a mixing bowl and whisk to combine. Dip both sides of sliced bread in custard mixture and place on heated waffle iron for 2-3 minutes until bread has a waffle-like texture.

To plate: Place the "waffle" on center of plate in a layered style and drizzle with maple syrup, powdered sugar and berries.

During my days as a broke line cook-bachelor, I only had a George Foreman grill in my apartment. One day I discovered that French toast actually came out better this way. When I was able to purchase a waffle iron, I was able to create something truly amazing. This will definitly bring WOW to your brunch.

Gingerbread Pancakes

Serves 4

1¼ cup	All purpose flour
3 tsps	Baking powder
as needed	Sugar and salt
1 cup	Coffee (fresh brewed)
2 tbs	Butter (melted) (plus extra for cooking)
1 tsp	Ginger powder
1 tsp	Fresh ginger (minced)
1 tsp	Crystallized ginger (minced)

Stir together dry ingredients and add coffee, melted butter and all gingers. Stir together until combined. Cook on hot griddle or nonstick frying pan until nicely brown on both sides.

To plate: Stack three medium pancakes on a plate and drizzle with honey or your favorite syrup. Top with whipped cream, berries and crystallized ginger.

To this day I use this recipe to "show off" when I need to make pancakes. I learned this back in my college days working in a diner in NYC during the weekends. This was always a hit on the menu. BTW, all celebrated chefs have worked at a diner or similar establishment at some point in their lives.

Eggs Florentine

Serves 2

Florentine Sauce

1 tsp	Butter
1 tsp	Flour
1 cup	Milk
a pinch	Nutmeg
1 cup	Spinach (roughly chopped)
cup	Grated gouda, mozzarella (mixed)
2 ozs	Cream cheese
as needed	Salt and pepper

Poached Eggs

4	Eggs (large)
1 tbs	White vinegar
as needed	Water
2	English muffin (sliced and toasted)

In a saucepan, melt butter and the flour to make a roux. Add milk gradually (one quarter cup at a time), whisking continously until there are no lumps, and sauce thickens. Add nutmeg, spinach and cheeses. Continue whisking over a low heat until the cheeses have melted. Adjust seasoning with salt and pepper. Hold warm until ready for use.

In a shallow pan, bring enough water to the simmer, add vinegar. Do not let water boil.

Carefully break each egg into a bowl. Then, one at a time, drop eggs into simmering water and poach for 3-5 minutes. Remove from water with a slotted spoon and place on top of half an English muffin.

To plate: Place two (half) muffins with poached eggs on a plate and spoon Florentine sauce over. Garnish with chopped bacon, smoked salmon or your favorite condiment.

This is pulled up from my childhood. Indian spiced potatoes folded between a wheat dough and cooked on "thawa" or griddle and served with yogurt. This is serious Sunday brunch munch.

My Mom's Aloo ki Roti (Potato Stuffed Roti)

Makes 2 to 3 rotis

1 cup	Whole wheat flour
½ cup	Water
1	Potato
¼ cup	Red onion (finely minced)
as needed	Salt
as needed	Cayenne pzpper
½ tsp	Garam masala

½ tsp	Cumin seeds
1/8 cup	Cilantro (chopped)
a squeeze	Lime
½	Green chili, optional (finely chopped)
as needed	Olive oil for frying

Combine flour and water to make dough. Knead for five minutes. Form dough into equal sized balls. Cover with a towel and let rest.

Prick holes into the potato with a fork, and microwave for 4-5 minutes until soft. Peel and mash potato, then add the rest of seasonings, onions and cilantro. Make sure to taste potatoes for the correct saltiness.

Roll the roti into 4-5 inch circles and place one ice cream scoop of mash potato in the center of the roti. Fold upwards 8 times to completely cover the potato mixture.

Flatten roti with your hand then gently roll back out into a 4-5 inch circle.
Cook on both sides, like a pancake, in a non-stick frying pan until brown.

Brush both sides with olive oil, and cook a little more on each side until golden and slightly crispy on outside.

This is great served with yogurt or your favorite salsa and makes an interesting addition to a Sunday brunch or luncheon.

Stuffed French Toast
with Cream Cheese and Caramelized Pecans

Serves 2

1	Extra thick slice of brioche
½ cup	Cream cheese (at room temperature)
½ cup	Caramelized pecans, finely chopped (see page 182)
¼ cup	Honey
1 cup	Milk
3	Eggs
2 tbs	Sugar
1 tsp	Vanilla extract
2 oz	Grand Marnier (optional)
1 tbs	Butter
as needed	Powdered sugar
as needed	Honey, maple syrup or crème anglaise
as needed	Berries, bananas or fruit

Slice brioche in half and hollow out as shown in the picture. Make filling by combining cream cheese, pecans and honey in a mixing bowl. Stuff brioche with this mixture and set aside until ready to use.

In another mixing bowl, combine milk, eggs, sugar, vanilla and Grand Marnier, mix all ingredients well. Dip stuffed brioche in the egg mixture and make sure it absorbs nicely. Place the brioche on a hot griddle or frying pan with some butter. Do not let it burn. Cooking times and heat level will vary according to how thick you sliced your bread and how long you soaked it in the egg mixture.

Once cooked, drizzle with your favorite sauce, berries and powdered sugar and enjoy!

Ask your baker for an unsliced loaf of brioche so that you can slice it as thick as you want. I like to go two inches. This was also a hit in the "Dino's Bistro" days. Be creative with the sauces, use flavored honeys or syrups, berries or crème Anglaise. It is impossible to not make this taste good.

3 cups	Rolled oats
1 cup	Slivered almonds
1 cup	Pistachios
¾ cup	Sweetened, shredded coconut flakes
1/3 cup	Dark brown sugar
1/3 cup	Maple syrup
¼ cup	Vegetable oil
1 tsp	Salt
1 cup	Dried cranberries

Pre-heat oven to 350º F.

Combine all the ingredients, except the dried cranberries, in a mixing bowl and spread on a baking tray. Place in the oven to roast.

After 15-20 minutes remove from oven and let them cool completely on the baking tray. Once cooled transfer to a bowl and add the dried cranberries. You can store in ziplock bags for up to two weeks.

This can be served over ice cream, or as we have shown here with Greek yogurt, honey and berries.

Who said yummy can't be healthy. Greek yogurt with honey is one of my personal favorite all time snack foods. When you add the combination of nuts or dried fruit, it becomes something truly special, and packed with beneficial nutrients. This is a great breakfast, brunch or dessert item.

Potato Pancakes

Serves 4-6

3	Russet Potatoes	¼ cup	Flour
1	Onion	as needed	Salt, pepper and olive oil
2	Eggs		

Grate potatoes and onion into a mixing bowl. Drain off any excess liquid, then add eggs, flour, salt and pepper and mix well. Heat a skillet over medium-high heat. Add olive oil, spoon mixture into pan to form pancakes. Cook 2-3 minutes or until golden brown, then flip over and continue to cook for another 2 minutes.

You can serve this with so many things from sautéed mushrooms, caramelized onions, sour cream, smoked salmon, bacon, poached eggs.

I make this as a side order for steaks sometimes for special NYC guests at the restaurant. They have officially given me the stamp of approval, endorsing these potato pancakes as NYC worthy. (Don't know if that's a compliment or not). Maybe NYC potato pancakes wish they could be St. Maarten worthy!!!

Ricardo Wyatt | Do-Re-Me-Fa-So-La-Ti

Caribbean Cornucopia

Pass through the portal of passion,
poured into sweet paradise.

Taste in Caribbean fashion,
sugar-filled sun-dipped delights!

Fanciful ornaments sway merrily on trees.
Red pomegranates dance to the breeze.

Yellow passion fruits drop in the shade,
for morningside gathering when Maracuja is made.

Tall island cane harvests boil down to molasses,
while brown sugar ferments to put rum in our glasses.

Guava and Belle Apples stewed gold in a pot,
dress cold ice cream and best served while still hot!

Mangoes, bananas, star apples, papaya,
delectables soak bottled to flavor rum's fire.

The twittering and buzzing of birds and the bees,
busily gathering to sow tiny seeds,
as tropical pleasures birth in the sun,
the flowers of life have again just begun.

Poem by Laura Richardson

Flamboyant Bouquet with Sea Grapes, Mangoes, Cashews and Potatoes
Original Oil painted from life by Sir Roland Richardson | 29 inches x 29 inches | April 2002

¼ cup	Pine nuts
¼ cup	Parmigiano Reggiano
2 cloves	Garlic
as needed	Salt and pepper

Combine all ingredients in a food processor and pulse until almost smooth.

Tomato Sauce

Yield 2 cups

as needed	Olive oil
1	Onion (diced)
2 cloves	Garlic (minced)
2 cans	Cherry tomatoes (4 cups approximately)
6-8 leaves	Fresh basil
as needed	Salt, pepper and sugar
1 wedge	Lemon

1. Sweat onions and garlic together in a large pot, add tomatoes and bring to a boil. Reduce heat to low and cook sauce at a simmer.
2. Pour sauce into a blender using a few quick pulses to puree.
3. Return to pot and add one squeeze of lemon, and hold warm until ready to use.

Yield 1 qt

2	Onion (sliced)
1 bunch	Fresh thyme
4 cloves	Garlic (minced)
as needed	Olive oil
½ bottle	Red wine
2 cups	Demi-glace

1. Sautee onions, thyme and garlic with olive oil in a pot on medium heat until caramelized. Follow same process as for making onion soup. The caramelization of the onions is key for fully developed flavor.
2. Add the wine and demi-glace and bring to a simmer. Let reduce by 25% and chill as fast as you can. This sauce will last for 3-4 days once properly chilled.
   This is a great sauce to braise anything, from osso bucco, to short ribs or lamb shanks.

Sundried Tomato "Tapenade"

Yield 3 cups

1 cup	Sundried tomatoes (not the ones in oil)
2 cloves	Garlic
1 bunch	Basil
as needed	Olive oil
1 cup	White wine
2 cups	Heavy cream

1. In a saucepan, add sundried tomatoes, garlic and basil. Let simmer until tomatoes are soft.
2. Add white wine and cream and cook until cream is reduced.
3. Place sauce in a blender or food processor and puree until smooth.
   This is great to flavor any pasta sauce or spread on toast for a bruschetta.

Peppercorn Sauce

Yield 2 cups

½ cup	Mixed peppercorns (black, white, green, pink)
1 clove	Garlic (minced)
1 cup	Cognac
2 cups	Demi-glace
as needed	Heavy cream and to finish

1. In a saucepan, combine peppercorns, garlic and cognac and let this reduce "au sec". The idea here is to infuse peppercorns with the cognac flavor. Add demi-glace and bring to a simmer.
2. Before serving, finish sauce with heavy cream and butter.

Mushroom Sauce

Yield 1 qt

2 lbs	Assorted mushrooms (white, portabello, morels, chanterelles)
2 cloves	Garlic (minced)
as needed	Olive oil
1 qt	Heavy cream
as needed	Salt and white pepper
2 oz	Ketjap Manis
½ bunch	Fresh tarragon

1. In a rondeau or wide frying pan, sauté mushrooms and garlic with olive oil until soft.
2. Add cream, Ketjap Manis, seasonings and tarragon. Simmer over low heat. Hold warm until ready to use.

Pad Thai Sauce

Yield 1 qt

as needed	Sesame oil
as needed	Pomace olive oil
¼ cup	GGS (equal parts ginger-garlic-scallions minced)
2 tbs	Green curry paste
2 cans	Coconut milk (approximately 1 qt)
1 tbs	Peanut butter
¼ cup	Cilantro, mint, basil (roughly chopped)

In saucepan, heat sesame and olive oils. Add GGS and sauté quickly for 1 minute until flavors released. Add the rest of the ingrediants and bring to a simmer.

Citrus Glaze

Yield 3 cups

1 cup	Frozen orange juice
½ cup	Orange marmalade
1 cup	Hoisin sauce
2 tbs	Rice wine vinegar
2 tbs	Pickled ginger
¼ cup	Kumquats

Combine all ingredients in a blender. Use as a glaze for duck, chicken or fish while grilling.

Asian Glaze (for Grilling)

Yield 2 cups

1 cup	Citrus glaze
1 cup	Ketjap Manis

Combine both sauces in mixing bowl. Set aside until ready to use. This is great for brushing on grilled shrimps, meats, chicken, tuna and duck.

Mashed Potatoes

Yield 6 Servings

5	Idaho Potatoes (peeled and cut into 4-5 pieces)
½ cup	Milk
1 cup	Heavy cream
2 sprigs	Fresh rosemary
1 stick	Butter
as needed	Salt and pepper

Boil potatoes until fork tender, drain and set in a large mixing bowl.

Bring cream, milk , butter and rosemary to a boil. Slowly add to potatoes while mashing using a potato masher.

Substitute sweet potatoes or purple potatoes for variation.

Once all combined. Whip the potatoes using a whisk until light and airy. Mashed potatoes will appear lighter and thinner than normal. Let it rest for one hour and you will have perfect mashed potatoes, as the starches will continue to absorb the liquids.

Basil Oil

Yield 1 qt

2 bunches	Fresh basil
as needed	Salt and pepper
2 cloves	Garlic
3 cups	Olive oil
½ cup	Parmesan cheese (shredded)

Combine all ingredients in a blender and blend until smooth. Use this for a dipping sauce for bread, for decorating plates and to sauté potatoes.

Balsamic Dressing/Vinaigrette

Yield 1qt

2 tbs	Honey
1 cup	Balsamic vinegar
½ cup	Hazel nut oil (optional)
2 cups	Olive oil (not extra virgin)
½ cup	Extra virgin olive oil
1 tbs	Dijon mustard
1 sprig	Rosemary
as needed	Salt and pepper

Place all ingredients, except rosemary, in a blender. Blend until just combined. Pour into a container with the rosemary sprig. Keep in fridge for up to two months. Use as needed.

Garlic Butter

Yield 1 cup

2 sticks	Butter (softened)
10 cloves	Garlic (minced)
1 bunch	Parsley (minced)
as needed	Salt and pepper

In a small bowl, combine softened butter, minced garlic and parsley. Season with salt and pepper. This is great to melt into sauces, sauté vegetables or pastas.

Truffle Butter

Yield 1 cup

2 sticks	Butter (softened)
½ cup	Truffle tapenade (store bought)

In a small bowl, combine softened butter and tapenade, season with salt, mix well. This is great to sauté vegetables, to melt into sauces or to melt over baked potatoes.

Caramelized Nuts

Yield 2 cups

2 cups	Pecan, walnuts , hazelnuts or pistachios
2 cups	Simple syrup (equal parts of sugar and water)
pinch	Salt

1. Bring all ingredients to a boil in a sauce pan and let simmer.
2. Remove nuts from the liquid and place on a nonstick baking sheet.
3. Bake in a 350°F oven for 10 minutes or until toasted.

Chocolate Ganache

Yield 2 cups

1 cup	Heavy cream
2 cups	Best quality dark chocolate (chopped or chips)

Bring heavy cream to boil and pour over chocolate. Cover with plastic wrap and let sit for five minutes to let the chocolate melt on its own. With a whisk, stir gently until chocolate and cream are emulsified.

When warm it is a great chocolate sauce. When cold it can be used to make truffles, mousses and fillings. This is very versatile.

Shallot Marmalade

Yield 2 cups

2 cups	Shallots (thinly sliced)
1 cup	White vinegar
1 cup	Sugar

Bring all ingredients to a boil in a small pan, and cook until almost all moisture has evaporated and shallots have taken on a deep golden color.   Use this to enhance sauces or as a topping for foie gras or steak. Don't be afraid to use different flavored vinegars

Caramel Sauce

Yield 1 qt

1 stick	Butter
3 cups	Sugar
1 cup	Heavy cream (heated)

Melt butter, add sugar, and let sugar melt and eventually turn brown. When most of the sugar has become a dark rich brown color, stir quickly with a wooden spoon to make sure all sugar crystals have melted. Add heated cream. Be careful, it will splatter and bubble, but will settle. Let cool.

Chimichurri Sauce

Yield 2 cups

1 bunch	Parsley
5 cloves	Garlic
1 cup	Olive oil
½ cup	White vinegar
as needed	Salt, sugar and pepper

Finely chop parsley and garlic and mix in the rest of the ingredients.

Pickled Red Onions

Yield 2 cups

3	Red onions (thinly sliced)
2 cups	White vinegar
1 cup	Water
1 cup	Equal parts salt, peppercorns, coriander seeds and sugar

Slice onions paper thin. Set aside. Combine rest of ingredients and pour over onions. Place overnight in refrigerator. Serve on top of grilled meats, burgers, kebabs or salads.

Coconut Curry Sauce

Yield 4 cups

as needed	Olive oil
1 cup	Onion (roughly chopped)
2 cups	Tomatoes (roughly chopped)
4 cloves	Garlic (minced)
3 tbs	Ginger (minced)
1 tsp	Garam masala
1 tsp	Ground cumin
1 tsp	Tumeric powder
2 tbs	Coriander powder
as needed	Cayenne pepper (depending on how hot you like it)
1 cup	Water
½ cup	Toasted cashews
3 cups	Coconut milk
½ tsp	Mustard seeds
¼ cup	Fresh cilantro

Add olive oil to a large sauté pan over high heat. Add onions, tomatoes, ginger and garlic. Cook the aromatics until they start to sweat and become soft. Add spices and continue to cook until the flavors of the spices have been released. Add water and bring to a simmer.

Add the cashews and coconut milk. Then blend and puree the sauce until smooth.

In another sauté pan, over a high heat, add some more olive oil and mustard seeds. Wait until they start to pop. Then fry the sauce in this mixture. This is called "giving Tarkha," which is essentially releasing the flavors of the sauce. Your sauce is now ready.

Caesar Dressing

Yield 2 cups

1½ cup	Mayonnaise
1 tbs	Anchovy paste
¼ cup	Balsamic vinegar
1 tbs	Dijon mustard
2 tbs	Lemon juice
as needed	Salt and pepper

Mix all ingredients in a bowl until well combined. This will keep for two weeks in the fridge.

Ice Cream

Yield 1 qt

2 cups	Heavy cream
1 cup	Sweetened condensed milk
1 cup	Milk
as needed	Sugar (to your desired level of sweetness)
as needed	Flavoring of your choice : vanilla, bananas, strawberries, peanut butter, chocolate, maple syrup, ginger, bacon bits, chopped nuts, fresh basil, chocolate chips are all great ideas

Prepare the base and add sugar to your desired sweetness. Add any flavor you wish as well. Freeze in an ice cream batch freezer until smooth. Be careful not to over churn the ice cream as it will become grainy. Freeze immediately until set(approximately two hours). This is a great base that is also eggless and it saves a lot of time rather than having to make a custard.

Balsamic-Soy Reduction

Yield 1 cup

2 cups	Balsamic vinegar
1 cup	Soy sauce
1 cup	Sugar

Bring all ingredients to a boil and reduce by 75%, or until it is a thick syrup the consistency of molasses. This is great to drizzle on top of stir fries, or Asian dishes for an intense pop, an unexpected zing. We use this to perk up our version of Pad Thai, which traditionally calls for tamarind.

Shellfish Broth

Yield 2 qts

as needed	Olive oil
1 cup	Fresh tomatoes
8 cups	Shrimp shells, lobster shells, mussel shells.
1 cup	White wine
10 cups	Water
1 bunch	Tarragon and parsley

Saute tomatoes and shellfish shells. Add white wine, water, tarragon and parsely. Bring to a boil and then let simmer for one hour. Strain and cool immediately.

Blend all ingredients. Strain and pour into a squeeze bottle. This sauce will last for weeks. You can use this sauce as a dipping sauce for sushi, sashimi and chicken wings with the addition of some honey.

Tips, Silliness and Accidental Discoveries ...

Gold Medal Wine Geek!!!

Chocolate Cobbler ... yeah baby!!!"

Nothing fishy here ...

Virgin...like the olive oil!!!

Instant Creole Sauce!!!
Mix onion soup, marinara sauce and simmer. Add cilantro and chopped peppers.

Instant Chocolate Mousse!!!
High end chocolate ganache plus whipped cream. Low end, instant chocolate pudding with cool whip.

Try Outs!!!
Try curry sauce with pesto for great sauce for shrimps or scallops.

Try rice flour for frying. I use it for everything from fried calamari to French fries.

Super Secrets!!!
Equal parts ketchup, mayo and mustard with shallot marmalade make a great burger sauce or sauce for roasted or fried chicken, hot dogs or grilled cheese.

Go Easy!!!
Remember you can always add more to a dish, but once it's in, you can't take it out, so go easy!

More Try Outs!!!
Try flavored mustards and mayos etc, when you make sandwiches or salads. I love dill and tarragon mayo for chicken, tuna or potato salad.

Melted chocolate on rye toast ... yummmmmy!!!

Any cheese, nut and honey combo will always impress!

188

So fresh...
and pure!!!

Can't resist the
Temptation!!!"

Well balanced!!!

Stand clear... Zorro
in 'da house!!!

Think of foods differently to make them less intimidating. For example, think of Gazpacho as a "vegetable smoothie" instead of some elaborate soup.

Always save rendered fat from bacon, duck and foie gras. This is great for cooking potatoes, frying vegetables, spreading on toast or for salad dressings.

Life is short, go ahead and lick the cake batter from the bowl.

It's SIMPLE: great ingredients make great food, chefs are not magicians.

Get to know the chef, and you will start to enjoy dining out even more.

Cook pasta one minute less than the package directions, and the last minute in the sauce!

Fried chicken skin, coleslaw, French fries in a biscuit is a "crazy yummy "sandwich.

Prepare every meal with love, joy and good intentions.

Taste while you cook. Don't wait till the end. Taste and season every step of the way.

Recipes are Only a Guide, Not a Bible!!!

Feel free to substitute similar ingredients to suit your preference. For example try oregano instead of thyme, or apples instead of pears.

A sharp knife is a safe knife.

A damp towel placed under your cutting board will prevent it from sliding.

189

Potato Salad

Lord, give me potato salad for my funeral procession,
a fast salsa, rum punch for a happy reception!

Everything delicious, nothing denied,
to farewell this lifetime of vanity pride.

No further worries, no lasting regrets,
a moment of fun where we'll all place some bets,

A straight shot up, or hot slide down,
dust in the wind or dug deep in the ground.

No songs, please, no words of praise,
just rich and creamy mayonnaise,

and piles of potatoes, with lots of strong drink,
till all bellies are full and all cheeks have turned pink!

That's a day to look forward to,
melted butter on bread, tender meat raviolis,
chocolate fondu, pistachio canolis,

loaded with calories, with nothing to dread
in that moment I'm finally dead!

Poem by Laura Richardson

Flamboyant Bouquet with Potatoes and Rum Bottles
Original Oil painted from life by Sir Roland Richardson
22 inches x 28 inches | August 2014 | Cupecoy, St. Maarten

Two Portraits Come to Life in the Kitchen ...

"I mentioned to my wife Laura that I had seen Dino in the market and had suggested I do his portrait one day. This happened on more than one occasion. He and I only gave it that moment's thought, but Laura remembered and one day and called Dino.

"Laura, this is amazing!" He then explained that they were in the midst of doing his cookbook and as yet had no idea that satisfied them for the cover. "Maybe the portrait is the solution," Dino said. Both became very excited and the next thing I knew we were setting an appointment to paint his portrait.

In the first session, we got acquainted through a series of quick charcoal drawings. This opened the door to exploration and discovery. Eventually the composition revealed itself, the shape and size of the canvas, the idea started to come alive. We began the painting in his world, his kitchen. His father, mother, brother, niece, all of

the waiting staff, every member of his kitchen team, came to watch the transformation of a blank canvas into the presence of the Chef. Many guests also found themselves in the kitchen watching it happen, everyone's comments and interest, a source of encouragement to me. Mary and Laura also came and took photos.

Dino himself would come and go as he saw to the preparation and presentation of each meal, "to make sure that it is also beautiful on its dish." In one of our last sessions, it was just the two of us, quiet, very focused. The painting was almost finished but somehow not entirely. Something more was not yet there. Dino was called away to greet some guests/friends in the dining room. I continued to work on the paraphernalia in the kitchen: pots, hanging pans, dish stacks, bottles. I stood back to study the painting when movement caught my attention; my reflection in the mirrored hallway, standing at my easel. This view had been blocked when Dino was posing, standing with his arms crossed, in his foot-tall Chef's hat, blocking the doorway behind him.

Spontaneously, in rapid gesture, I painted my self-portrait. Now we were two in the picture. Upon his return, Dino saw it immediately and embraced this new development. He went even further. In a burst of inspiration, he decided he wanted his cookbook to be more than "flavors, savors and fine food." Now he imagined it filled also with my art and Laura's poetry; an art cookbook. He found what he had been seeking all along, to create something unique to be treasured by all.

From the beginning of painting, which means the history of mankind, until recently (a century and a half ago with the invention of the camera), portraiture has been the means by which the likeness, the mode of dress and life, the environment, the hopes and beliefs of humans, have been preserved and passed down to us. It is unique to the human species to make pictures of themselves. The antiquity of art is the greatest proof of its importance to us. Portraiture must therefore carry all that makes us human and that means foremost our preoccupation with the mystery of life which surrounds us and interpenetrates us. We know that the animating force of life is invisible and eternal, even though we are visible and transient. The art of the portrait addresses these inner characteristics, more than just the outer appearance."
Sir Roland Richardson

Portrait of Dino (Front Cover Portrait)
Original Oil painted from life by Sir Roland Richardson
44 inches x 34 inches | September 2013 | Cupecoy, St. Maarten

Sir Roland Richardson

Sir Roland Richardson has an amazing history on our beautiful St. Martin, which includes 300 years of family history dating back through the first European settlement and even earlier Amerindian culture. He is a descendent of slavery as well as nobility, and poignantly represents the unique blend of many races, many cultures, and many continents that has emerged unto itself, Caribbean, Creole.

Sir Roland's contributions span fifty years since his full-scholarship fine art education at the Hartford Art School with top honor, when he chose to return to his native soil to paint and record his world. Every artwork he creates is done on location from life. Today, Roland Richardson's contribution as a leading "Plein Air" Impressionist artist has earned great recognition. Over 100 one-man and group shows have toured with his work all over the globe, and his paintings are cherished in the collections of celebrated dignitaries, famous artists and corporate leaders of our times.

Sir Roland's inspiration extends beyond this, with a deep devotion of personal time and resources to the preservation of St. Martin's patrimony. As founding Editor-in-Chief of the popular island magazine, Discover St. Martin-St.Maarten, he diligently researched and documented many facets of St. Martin's history for the first time ever archived. His articles called forth professional archaeologists from Europe and the Caribbean to help uncover the island's past. His interviews with our elders have forever recorded oral history, woven with tales and myths, the times of old, as lessons for the new. Sir Roland was directly involved in central planning of both the French and Dutch museums on St. Martin. He was co-founder and President of the Cultural and Historic Foundation that

sponsored the island's first food festivals and ethnic performances, and offered vital support to many other community-driven foundations that continue these popular traditions today. Richardson's passions brought forth the restoration of Fort Louis, overlooking Marigot Harbor, where he worked tirelessly, encouraging other volunteers from the community to work together, to clear the steep path, and returned its ancient canons, which were helicoptered to their original home. They wrote the history, installed lighting, and built the same stairs that thousands of people have climbed to this magnificent overlook.

One of his finest contributions to our community's culture since 1998 is the Roland Richardson Gallery Museum. This magnificent venue in the Old Marie at #6 rue de la Republique, greets visitors six days a week. The 19th century Creole townhouse, fully restored, with its beautiful hidden courtyard garden, is surrounded by 18th century stone architecture that dates back before the French Revolution as the original barracks for the soldiers who came to build Fort Louis under the command of Chevalier de Durat, appointed by King Louis XVI.

Knighted in 2007 by the Court of Queen Beatrix of The Netherlands, Sir Roland Richardson has also been honored with several Lifetime Achievement Awards from the French Government.

Laura Richardson

Writing has always been a source of joy for me. As a child, I used to wake up with poems swirling in my head that poured onto paper right out of bed. I was privileged to work after school through high school as a page at our county library. On frozen, bleak days when no one ventured out, I quietly stole time in the poetry section lined with centuries of poets. There I wept in the aisle to poems that became lifetime favorites: Edna St. Vincent Millay's "Ballad of the Harp-Weaver", Edgar Allen Poe's "Annabel Lee", Robert Frost's "The Road Not Taken", and hundreds of others that opened my heart and my mind. Later, when it was time for university, I ventured to follow in Ms. Millay's footsteps and enrolled at Vassar College where I had read she spent her formative years writing.

Words transfixed me. Like fine perfume and musical notes

Looking back, I realize that was a critical turning point in my life. It was a time when language as a medium bloomed. Words transfixed me. Like fine perfume and musical notes, they had a vibrant quality all their own, filled with color and cadence and passion. Hours working in the school's Art History library opened a parallel door that eventually led to my many years as a gallery owner and art consultant. Through my work, I met my husband, artist Roland Richardson, whose Caribbean artworks are truly beacons of light, touching every continent around the world. I am honored that he gives me full choice among the vast treasures in his portfolio to illustrate my poems.

All of these poems have been written on the island of St. Martin, my husband's birth place, where we are now living together almost twenty years. The Richardson family is among the founding families of St. Martin from the 1700's. I've learned through my marriage, the uniqueness of their West Indian culture and traditions. I hope this little compilation of poems offers you a glimpse of the profound and abundant beauty that defines Paradise to me.

Be The Change Foundation

Be The Change Foundation's mission is to encourage the island community to actively contribute to various non-profit organizations and local initiatives by igniting a social philanthropic movement with our online crowd funding platform. Abiding by the saying "making every dollar count", our goal is to urge the masses to not only sign onto the program by donating anywhere from $1 and up monthly or annually, but to also volunteer their time. This collective effort to raise funds and awareness for the various causes we feature will help create constant and long-term social change where it is is most needed, leading to a more united island community.

Art Saves Lives Foundation

Art Saves Lives Foundation established January 2013 promotes a cross-cultural exchange between youth in need and experienced practicing artists who seek to use their talents for positive change. This collaborative project selects renowned artists from around the world who use the arts to introduce participants to global and local traditions and empower them with the life skills necessary to effectively deal with the demands and challenges of everyday life. The program also provides guidance for young artists with aspirations in pursuing a career in the arts.

Yoga Class taught by **Kristina Blunt** | **Shakira Marshall** taught **Afro Soca Dance** | **Journey to Life's Balance Class** taught by **Hallemah Nash**

197

In closing ...

The restaurant business, while it can be very rewarding and has its obvious perks like "free food" and "open bar everyday" (for me, and my nearest and dearest), has its trials and tribulations, and its not so glamorous dark side. This business is full of unsung heroes. All the wait staff, sous chefs, cleaners, administrators, cashiers, bus boys, prep cooks, line cooks work under stressful conditions, do physically demanding work and, receive very little, if any, praise for their efforts. I salute every one of my employees for their commitment, hard work and dedication. It is your effort that contributes to the successes we have shared, and will continue to enjoy for years to come. I will always be grateful to the unsung heroes behind the scenes.

I owe Warren Sheppell and Morris Bershard a ton of gratitude, for not only believing in my talents as a chef, but also for the financial boost to get me going on my way to entrepreneurship. Over the years Temptation has accomplished all there is to accomplish in the St. Maarten dining scene, from numerous "Restaurant of the Year" awards from multiple media outlets, to gold medals at various competitions. We have received so many accolades and honorable mentions, have had the honor to serve innumerable celebrities, dignitaries and world leaders, from his Majesty King Willem Alexander of The Netherlands to Virgin's Sir Richard Branson.

Yet, the greatest achievement I credit to the restaurant is that it has kept the nucleus of my family together. Running a restaurant is at times a very stressful undertaking requiring a strong temperament. Before I opened, I made my mom work as a waitress in another restaurant so she could understand how short tempered the chef could be, and better understand the fine line between being a passionate

> I made my mom work as a waitress in another restaurant so she could understand how short tempered the chef could be

A family that eats together, and laughs together, STAYS together!

professional and a jerk. Thankfully, Temptation has kept the bond between my divorced parents stronger, they have learned to respect and value each other in spite of their differences. From hosting to cashiering and bookkeeping, having my parents there is a huge moral support for me.

As great as any chef is, and as great as the food that comes out of the kitchen is, no restaurant can be a success without a well run dining room. This is a people business and without hospitality you won't be in business. Those who know Temptation also know Asha, my mom, and it is no secret that without her efforts, energy and support there would be no Temptation. She deserves equal, if not more, credit for the success of the restaurant than I do. While I am known as "the boss", as a mom (my mom and Temptation's mom), she

Shane

"The curve of a smile can set a lot of things straight."

will always be the "big boss". I am beyond grateful to have her as my mom, and part of my team at the restaurant. My brother Arun used to drop my name when he needed a favor, a contact, or an appointment with someone important. Over the years he has evolved into creating his own successful life, and I owe him a ton of gratitude for being a brother I can use to get advice on business and marketing related matters. Now I drop his name when I need a favor, a contact, or an appointment with someone important.

I am also forever grateful towards Gulu chacha, and Meena chachi who taught me to challenge myself, and instilled a sense of discipline in me that has helped me throughout my life.

Thankfully with a great education at the Culinary Institute of America, and great industry mentors like Patrick Duff,

Anna

"Excellence is not a matter of chance, it's a matter of choice."

201

202

Alain Kandaperredy, Mark Harris, Jeff Masek, Mickhael Pacary, Marie Fagan, Johnnie Correa, Craig Spann, and my dad the famous "Mr Jack" I have been able to mold an amazing career, and have had, and will continue to have, a blast doing so.

I owe Bryan Le Compte a big high five, for giving me the "butt kick" I needed to make this book happen, and even though this project has evolved many times over, Roland, Laura and myself are extremely proud with what we have created, and give a big kudos to Mary Wrigley, Richard James and Nataly Dannenberg for their efforts, talent, beautiful graphics, design and photography work that makes this book so worth having.

I hope that everyone who reads this book will get some gratification out of it, whether you are a foodie who wants

Tony

"It's kinda fun to do the IMPOSSIBLE ."
Walt Disney

to try my Chimichurri recipe (page 183) or you unexpectedly reinforce your appreciation of how colorfully alluring life can be by admiring the Baie Longe Colors III painting (page 40) and feel transported when you read its accompanying poem "Without Complaint".

So from the guy who has never read a book cover to cover in his life (including Cliffs Notes), I now present myself to you as a published author and in closing, I leave you with my mom's recipe for infinite happiness … a simple recipe she would like to share with you all, a recipe which can, and should, be enjoyed by all.

Remember to celebrate living by eating with flavor, and loving with flavor … cheers, and bon appetite.

Priya

"Focusing on the good."

203

... at the market in Marigot

"Nothing great was
ever achieved without
enthusiasm"
Ralph Waldo Emmerson

"Coming together is the beginning. Keeping together is progress. Working together is SUCCESS. *Henry Ford*

Temptation's Mantra:
"Strive for excellence, not perfection"

Recipe for infinite *happiness*

Serves everyone

You will need equal amounts of the following

infinite	*peace*
infinite	*love*
infinite	*health*
infinite	*wisdom*
infinite	*harmony*
infinite	*sunlight*
infinite	*gratitude*